TOTALLY RANDOM

QUESTIONS

VOLUME 1

101 Wild and Weird Q&As

Contents

About how many stars exist in the universe?

a. 100 million

b. 100 trillion

c. 1 septillion

ANSWER: **c**

1 septillion

FROM EARTH, THE MILKY WAY—THE GALAXY THAT CONTAINS OUR SOLAR SYSTEM—looks like a hazy band of light swirling across the night sky. With the use of telescopes on Earth and in space, astronomers have figured out that the Milky Way contains about 100 billion stars—a number so large it's hard to imagine. And, even more amazing, **the Milky Way is just one of at least 10 trillion galaxies** in our universe, according to astronomers. How can we estimate the total number of stars in the whole universe, then? Astronomers take the number of stars in the Milky Way and multiply that by the number of galaxies. The answer? One septillion stars. That's **1,000,000,000,000,000,000,000,000!**

Instant Genius
The Milky Way is a spiral-shaped galaxy.

True or False:

A sneeze
blows out of your nose at 10 miles an hour (16 kmh).

#2

ANSWER: True

WHEN SOMETHING IRRITATING SUCH AS DIRT, POLLEN, SMOKE, OR DUST ENTERS YOUR NOSTRILS, it may tickle the tiny hairs and delicate skin that line the inside of your nose. The presence of these tiny intruders sends an **electric signal** to your brain that your nose needs to clear itself, and **your brain tells your body it's time for a sneeze.** Your body responds by preparing itself. This is when you stiffen up. **Within seconds,** your eyes close, your tongue moves to the roof of your mouth, and your muscles brace for the oncoming sneeze. Achoo!

NOW YOU KNOW!
A single sneeze can release 100,000 germs into the air. That's why it's always good to catch your sneezes in a tissue or an elbow instead of in your hands.

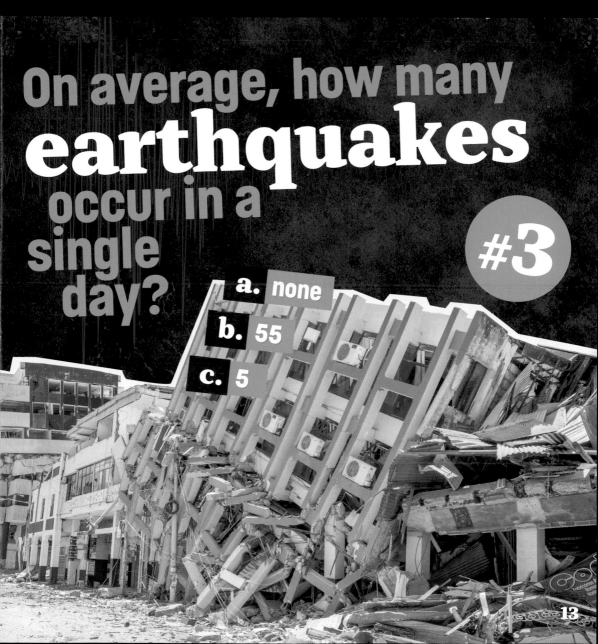

On average, how many **earthquakes** occur in a single day?

#3

a. none
b. 55
c. 5

13

ANSWER: b   55

THERE ARE ABOUT 55 EARTHQUAKES PER DAY, though most are too small to notice. Earthquakes usually occur along the edges of **tectonic plates,** which are large slabs of rock that make up Earth's crust. These plates move about 1 to 2 inches (3 to 5 cm) per year—about **as fast as your fingernails grow.** Some earthquakes are caused when the edges of the plates get stuck and push against each other but can't move. This builds pressure. Once the pressure gets strong enough, the rocks break, causing the plates to shift. This **sudden release of energy** makes the ground shake—that's an earthquake.

Tectonic plates

Indonesia

Instant Genius

Indonesia has the most earthquakes of any country. Antarctica has the fewest of any continent.

Why are Major League Baseball umpires all required to wear black underwear?

#4

a. It is the one color all the teams can agree on.

b. The underwear is made from a special fabric that comes only in black.

c. They might split their pants during games.

They might split their pants during games.

IN BASEBALL, AN UMPIRE'S JOB IS TO MAKE SURE EVERYONE IS PLAYING BY THE RULES. An umpire also begins and ends games, makes judgment calls on plays, and disciplines players who have broken the rules. To keep their eye on the ball, **umpires spend a lot of time squatting,** bending over, and getting into **awkward positions.** This can cause the seams of their pants to split. If they do, black underwear makes it much less noticeable!

Instant Genius

It takes 7 to 10 years of training to become a professional Major League umpire.

#5

True or False:

A cloud can weigh more than an elephant.

17

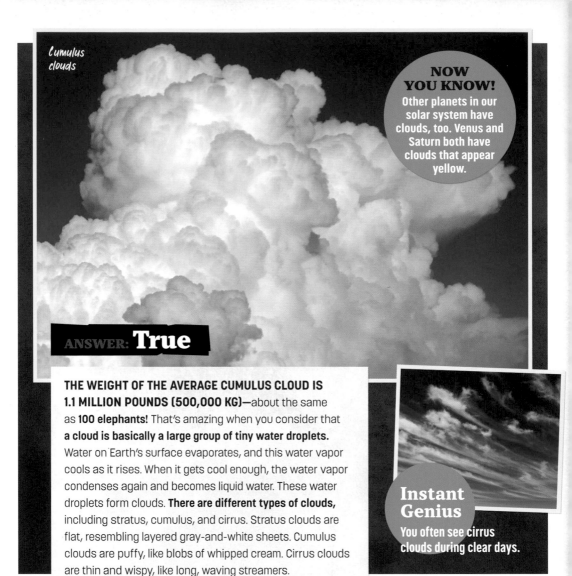

cumulus clouds

ANSWER: True

THE WEIGHT OF THE AVERAGE CUMULUS CLOUD IS 1.1 MILLION POUNDS (500,000 KG)—about the same as **100 elephants!** That's amazing when you consider that **a cloud is basically a large group of tiny water droplets.** Water on Earth's surface evaporates, and this water vapor cools as it rises. When it gets cool enough, the water vapor condenses again and becomes liquid water. These water droplets form clouds. **There are different types of clouds,** including stratus, cumulus, and cirrus. Stratus clouds are flat, resembling layered gray-and-white sheets. Cumulus clouds are puffy, like blobs of whipped cream. Cirrus clouds are thin and wispy, like long, waving streamers.

Instant Genius
You often see cirrus clouds during clear days.

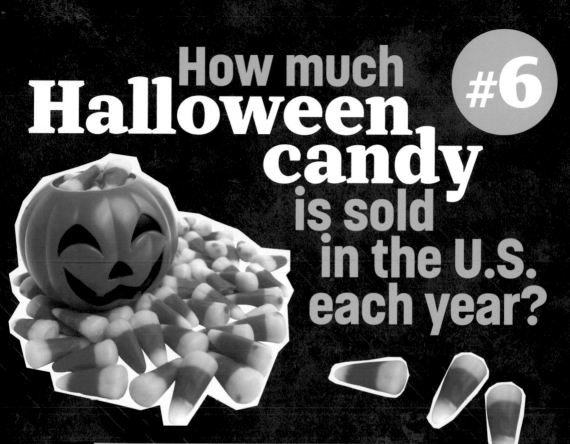

How much Halloween candy is sold in the U.S. each year?

a. 6 million pounds (2.7 million kg)

b. 60 million pounds (27 million kg)

c. 600 million pounds (272 million kg)

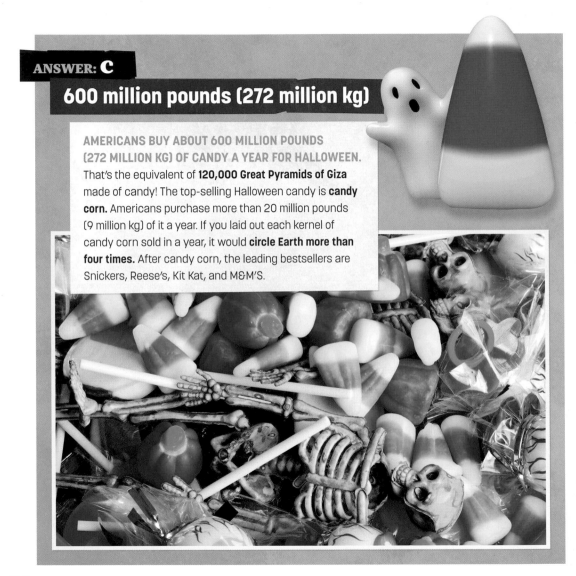

600 million pounds (272 million kg)

AMERICANS BUY ABOUT 600 MILLION POUNDS (272 MILLION KG) OF CANDY A YEAR FOR HALLOWEEN. That's the equivalent of **120,000 Great Pyramids of Giza** made of candy! The top-selling Halloween candy is **candy corn.** Americans purchase more than 20 million pounds (9 million kg) of it a year. If you laid out each kernel of candy corn sold in a year, it would **circle Earth more than four times.** After candy corn, the leading bestsellers are Snickers, Reese's, Kit Kat, and M&M'S.

Which of these mountains is the **highest in the world?**

a. **K2**

b. **Mount Everest**

c. **Mount Kangchenjunga**

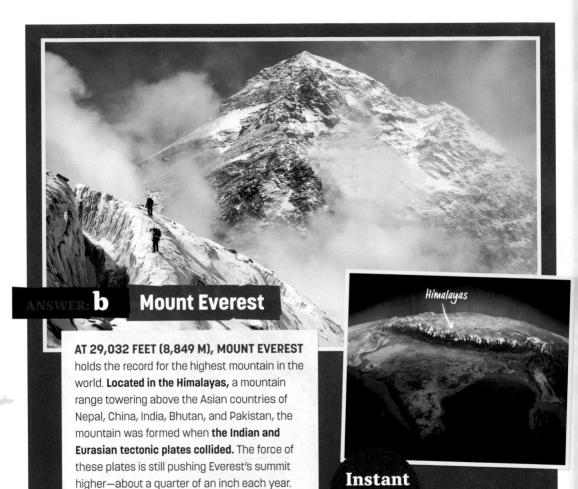

Himalayas

Mount Everest

AT 29,032 FEET (8,849 M), MOUNT EVEREST holds the record for the highest mountain in the world. **Located in the Himalayas,** a mountain range towering above the Asian countries of Nepal, China, India, Bhutan, and Pakistan, the mountain was formed when **the Indian and Eurasian tectonic plates collided.** The force of these plates is still pushing Everest's summit higher—about a quarter of an inch each year. With the peak of Everest reaching **above the clouds,** the mountain is frigid and can get very windy. From 17,400 feet (5,304 m) up, it is capped with snow and ice year-round.

Instant Genius

Winds on Mount Everest can reach up to 100 miles an hour (160 kmh).

#8

How
many
noses
does a
slug
have?

a. one **b.** four **c.** zero

ANSWER: **b** four

A SLUG HAS FOUR TENTACLES THAT IT USES TO MAKE SENSE OF ITS ENVIRONMENT. The upper pair, on its head, is sensitive to light and helps the slug see and smell. The lower pair, on the slug's face, helps it feel and taste. **It uses both pairs to detect food.** Slugs eat with a radula, which is a tongue-like body part covered with **thousands of tiny teeth called denticles.** Slugs breathe from a blowhole on the right side of their bodies that leads to **a single lung.**

NOW YOU KNOW!
Slugs produce a gooey mucus and leave a trail of slime wherever they go. The slime helps them slide forward and keeps them moist.

How can you tell the **difference** #9 between a crocodile and an alligator?

a. Compare their faces.

b. Compare their feet.

c. Compare their size.

Crocodile

Smile!

Alligator

I AM smiling!

ANSWER: **a**

Compare their faces.

IF YOU WANT TO TELL THESE REPTILES APART, JUST TAKE A LOOK AT THEIR SNOUTS. Crocodiles have **slender V-shaped snouts,** while the snouts of alligators are **wider and U-shaped.** When alligators close their mouths, you see only their upper teeth. Crocodiles, on the other hand, show a toothier grin, with both upper and lower teeth interlocking like a zipper. **The two are also different colors:** Crocodiles tend to be olive or tan, while alligators are usually black or tan.

True or False:

The deadliest tornado

on record happened on the continent of Antarctica.

TORNADOES HAVE HIT EVERY STATE IN THE UNITED STATES AND EVERY CONTINENT EXCEPT ANTARCTICA. A tornado is a rapidly spinning column of air that touches both the ground and a cloud above. **More than 1,000 tornadoes occur every year in the United States.** That's more than in any other country. The majority happen in two areas: **the state of Florida** and an area of the south-central U.S. nicknamed **Tornado Alley,** which includes the states of Texas, Oklahoma, Kansas, Nebraska, and South Dakota. Most tornadoes have wind speeds less than 100 miles an hour (160 kmh), but extreme tornadoes can reach winds of more than 300 miles an hour (480 kmh).

Instant Genius

An eight-year-old Alabama boy survived being sucked up by a tornado.

NOW YOU KNOW!

A tornado lasts from a few minutes to several hours, with the average touch-down time being five minutes.

Why don't woodpeckers get concussions?

a. They have small brains.

b. They know when to stop pecking.

c. Their skulls are protected by a natural seat belt.

#11

Now, that's using your head!

Their skulls are protected by a natural seat belt.

WOODPECKERS PECK TREES TO FIND INSECTS TO EAT, MARK THEIR TERRITORY, AND ATTRACT MATES. They may also peck to make a nesting site. But how can their little noggins take all that pecking? Woodpeckers have **skulls made of a sponge-like bone** that is built to spread out the impact of force. Every time the bird pecks, this bone acts like a seat belt for the bird's skull and the brain it protects. A woodpecker's brain also has **another layer of protection: the bird's tongue!** It wraps all the way around the skull providing more padding. Scientists think woodpeckers may provide some hints for how to make safer bike helmets.

Instant Genius

A woodpecker can peck really fast—about 20 times per second!

There are no volcanoes in space.

#12

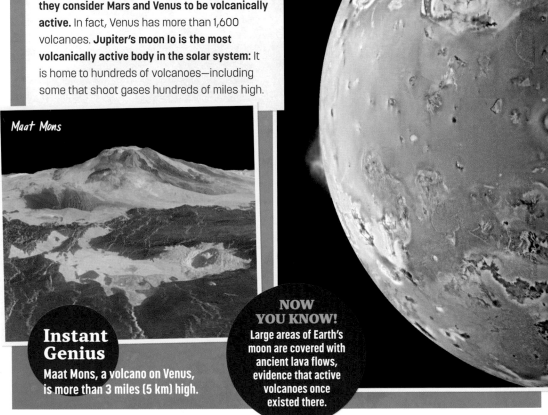

Jupiter's moon Io

ANSWER: False

VOLCANOES EXIST ON OTHER PLANETS AND MOONS IN OUR SOLAR SYSTEM. Although scientists have never witnessed an eruption, **they consider Mars and Venus to be volcanically active.** In fact, Venus has more than 1,600 volcanoes. **Jupiter's moon Io is the most volcanically active body in the solar system:** It is home to hundreds of volcanoes—including some that shoot gases hundreds of miles high.

Maat Mons

Instant Genius

Maat Mons, a volcano on Venus, is more than 3 miles (5 km) high.

NOW YOU KNOW!

Large areas of Earth's moon are covered with ancient lava flows, evidence that active volcanoes once existed there.

32

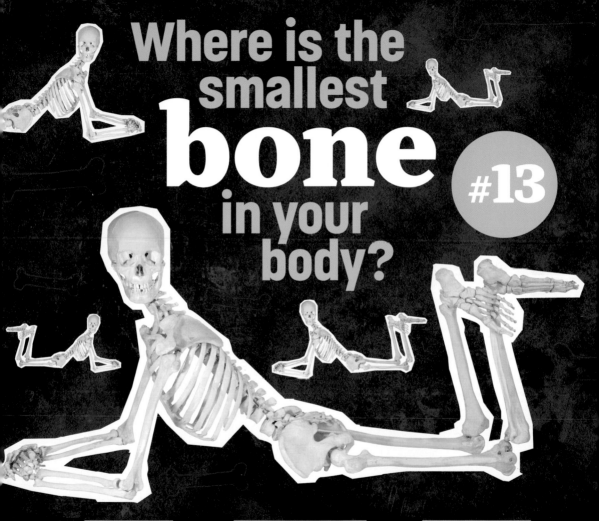

Where is the smallest **bone** in your body?

#13

a. your ear **b.** your little toe **c.** your pinky

33

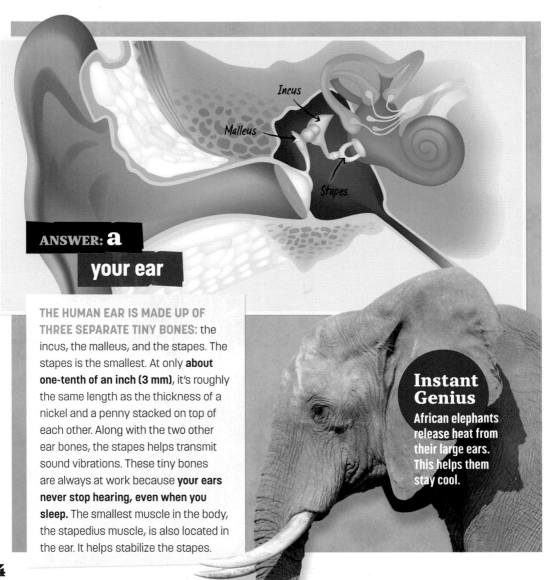

Incus

Malleus

Stapes

ANSWER: a

your ear

THE HUMAN EAR IS MADE UP OF
THREE SEPARATE TINY BONES: the
incus, the malleus, and the stapes. The
stapes is the smallest. At only **about
one-tenth of an inch (3 mm)**, it's roughly
the same length as the thickness of a
nickel and a penny stacked on top of
each other. Along with the two other
ear bones, the stapes helps transmit
sound vibrations. These tiny bones
are always at work because **your ears
never stop hearing, even when you
sleep.** The smallest muscle in the body,
the stapedius muscle, is also located in
the ear. It helps stabilize the stapes.

Instant Genius

African elephants
release heat from
their large ears.
This helps them
stay cool.

Which of the following can clean poisons in soil?

a. peanut butter

b. sunflowers

c. ice chips

ANSWER: b

sunflowers

IN ADDITION TO THEIR ABILITY TO BRIGHTEN UP A GARDEN, SUNFLOWERS ARE ALSO HYPERACCUMULATORS— plants that have the superpower to suck up poisons from soils **without getting poisoned themselves.** Sunflowers and other hyperaccumulators can pull the toxins from their roots to their leaves quickly, holding the toxins in the leaves to clean them. Sunflowers are **able to remove heavy metals,** such as arsenic, zinc, copper, and mercury. Soil scientists have discovered that sunflowers can also help **clean up nuclear waste** by sucking radiation out of the soil.

Instant Genius

Young sunflowers start the day facing east with the sunrise and move with the sun throughout the day.

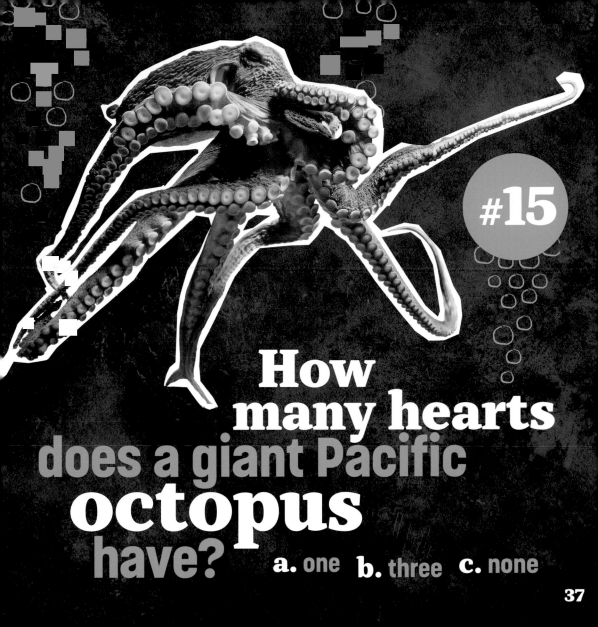

#15

How many hearts does a giant Pacific **octopus** have? **a.** one **b.** three **c.** none

ANSWER: **b** three

AN OCTOPUS HAS THREE HEARTS, AND EACH SERVES A DIFFERENT PURPOSE. A larger heart circulates blood throughout its body, while two smaller hearts pump blood to its gills. Like all octopuses, a giant Pacific octopus also has **nine brains:** a larger central brain to control its nervous system and additional smaller **brains in each of its eight arms to control movement.** This allows its arms to work independently or team up and work together. If an octopus loses an arm, no problem—it can just grow another one!

Instant Genius
Octopuses have blue blood.

38

Which is true about King Tut?

#16

a. He had a clubfoot.

b. He loved to hunt ostrich.

c. Both of the above.

39

ANSWER: **c**

Both of the above.

KING TUTANKHAMUN WAS A PHARAOH WHO RULED EGYPT FOR 10 YEARS UNTIL HIS DEATH, AT AGE 19. Not much was known about this young king until British archaeologist **Howard Carter discovered the pharaoh's tomb** about a hundred years ago. Tut's tomb contained more than 5,000 artifacts, including 130 walking sticks and paintings of the king seated during activities, all showing evidence of his clubfoot. The king was also buried with a fan made of ostrich feathers. The fan's handle showed the **king setting off in his chariot to hunt** the large birds on one side and returning with his prey on the other.

Howard Carter examining the sarcophagus from the tomb of King Tutankhamun

True or False:

There are **more species** of moths than butterflies.

#17

41

Butterfly

Moth

ANSWER: **True**

THERE ARE SOME 160,000 SPECIES OF MOTHS, COMPARED WITH "ONLY" 17,500 SPECIES OF BUTTERFLIES. Butterflies and moths have some unusual traits in common: They are the only group of insects that can coil up their feeding tube—a long, tongue-like part known as a proboscis (pro-BOSS-kiss). And, unlike other insects, they have scale-covered wings. **Butterflies and moths also have some key differences:** In general, butterflies are brightly colored and active during the day. Moths usually have duller colors and are active at night. The main difference between them is a good way to tell them apart: **Moths have feathery antennae, while butterflies' antennae are bulb-shaped at the top.**

NOW YOU KNOW!
The sunset moth from Madagascar is often considered the most beautiful in the world. Unlike many moth species, it is both colorful and active in the daytime.

What is
arachibutyrophobia?

a. the fear of needles

b. the fear of spiders

c. the fear of peanut butter sticking to the roof of your mouth

SINGLE USE ONLY

#18

43

ANSWER: C

the fear of peanut butter sticking to the roof of your mouth

FEAR IS A NATURAL HUMAN EMOTION TO ALERT US TO THE PRESENCE OF DANGER. Phobias are extreme fears related to specific situations. While many have experienced the surprise of a hunk of a peanut butter and jelly sandwich getting stuck to the roof of their mouths, usually a swig of milk or water is enough to take care of it. Those suffering from arachibutyrophobia (**a-ra-chi-bu-tyr-o-pho-bi-a**), however, are terrified of this happening to them. **They even wonder whether they will be able to survive it.** Some with this condition may be able to eat small amounts of peanut butter, while others will avoid eating peanut butter altogether.

True or False: There are no **green** land mammals.

#19

45

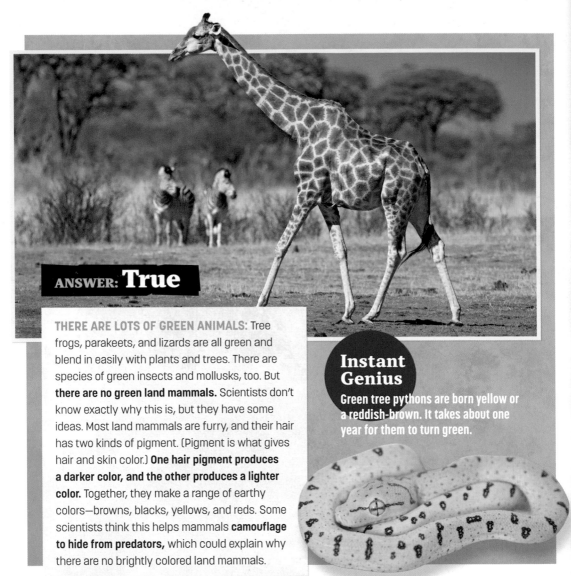

ANSWER: True

THERE ARE LOTS OF GREEN ANIMALS: Tree frogs, parakeets, and lizards are all green and blend in easily with plants and trees. There are species of green insects and mollusks, too. But **there are no green land mammals.** Scientists don't know exactly why this is, but they have some ideas. Most land mammals are furry, and their hair has two kinds of pigment. (Pigment is what gives hair and skin color.) **One hair pigment produces a darker color, and the other produces a lighter color.** Together, they make a range of earthy colors—browns, blacks, yellows, and reds. Some scientists think this helps mammals **camouflage to hide from predators,** which could explain why there are no brightly colored land mammals.

Instant Genius

Green tree pythons are born yellow or a reddish-brown. It takes about one year for them to turn green.

How many passengers survived the sinking of the RMS Titanic?

#20

a. none

b. less than one-third

c. half

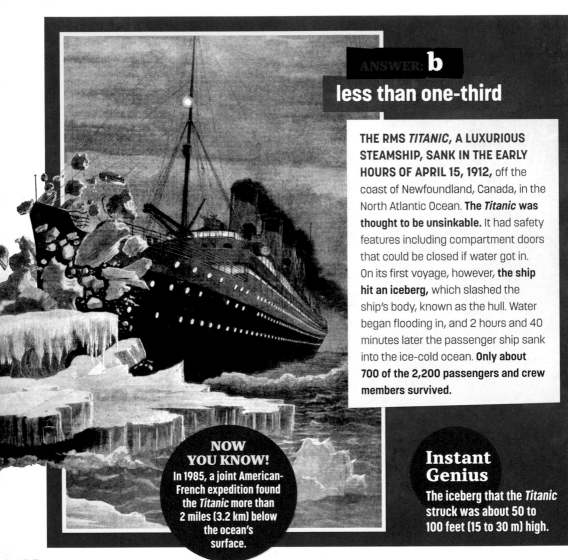

ANSWER: **b**

less than one-third

THE RMS *TITANIC*, A LUXURIOUS STEAMSHIP, SANK IN THE EARLY HOURS OF APRIL 15, 1912, off the coast of Newfoundland, Canada, in the North Atlantic Ocean. **The *Titanic* was thought to be unsinkable.** It had safety features including compartment doors that could be closed if water got in. On its first voyage, however, **the ship hit an iceberg,** which slashed the ship's body, known as the hull. Water began flooding in, and 2 hours and 40 minutes later the passenger ship sank into the ice-cold ocean. **Only about 700 of the 2,200 passengers and crew members survived.**

NOW YOU KNOW!

In 1985, a joint American-French expedition found the *Titanic* more than 2 miles (3.2 km) below the ocean's surface.

Instant Genius

The iceberg that the *Titanic* struck was about 50 to 100 feet (15 to 30 m) high.

What is a group of rhinoceroses called?

a. a herd

b. a crash

c. a pride

ANSWER: **b** **a crash**

MANY ANIMALS FORM SOCIAL GROUPS, AND THESE GROUPS HAVE NAMES THAT HELP IDENTIFY THEM. So why is a group of rhinoceroses called a crash? Well, **rhinos can weigh up to 1,500 pounds** (2,000 kg) and run faster than 30 miles an hour (48 kmh). **They also have poor eyesight.** Imagine these heavy mammals blindly barreling full steam ahead toward each other with their pointy horns and you have your answer. Yikes!

Instant Genius
A group of giraffes is called a tower.

What is a cucumber?

#22

a. a fruit

b. a vegetable

c. neither a fruit nor a vegetable

ANSWER: a

a fruit

BOTANISTS (SCIENTISTS WHO STUDY PLANTS) HAVE PARTICULAR DEFINITIONS for what makes something a fruit and what makes it a vegetable. **A fruit grows from the flower of a plant and has seeds.** A vegetable grows from other parts of the plant, such as the roots, stems, bulbs, or leaves, and it does not have seeds. Since cucumbers grow from the flower of the plant and have seeds, cucumbers are categorized as fruit. **Peppers, pumpkins, and tomatoes are also considered fruits** because they all have seeds.

Instant Genius

Fruits and veggies provide energy to help you think, move, and run.

Where do **flamingos** get their pink color from?

a. the food they eat

b. the water they drink

c. the sun

the food they eat

FLAMINGO CHICKS ARE BORN GRAY WITH WHITE FEATHERS. Over the course of about two years, they turn an orangey-pink. **Their color comes from beta-carotene** found in the algae, larvae, and tiny brine shrimp they eat. **Flamingos that live at a zoo will turn white** if their diet isn't supplemented with beta-carotene. This substance is also **what makes pumpkins and carrots orange.** Beneath the flamingo's wings, its feathers are black. The feathers are only seen when flamingos are flying.

Instant Genius

A group of flamingos is called a flamboyance.

#24

What is the planet **Mercury** made mostly of?

a. gas   b. iron   c. rings

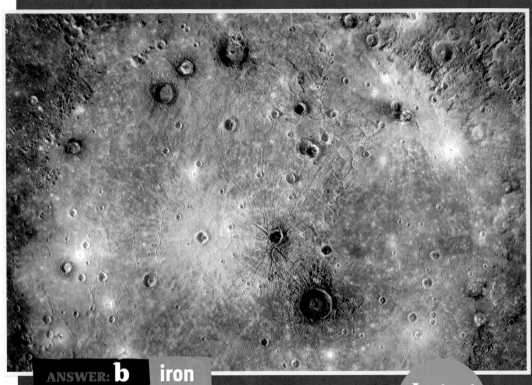

ANSWER: **b** iron

LIKE EARTH, MERCURY HAS A SOLID SURFACE MADE UP OF ROCKS OR METALS. Mercury also contains **the most iron of any planet in the solar system.** Its core, which is about the size of Earth's moon, is all iron. Being the closet planet to the sun means **Mercury also has the shortest orbit:** a superspeedy 88 days. By contrast, it takes Earth 365 days to go once around the sun, and Neptune—the farthest planet from the sun—takes 165 years!

Instant Genius

Like Earth's moon, Mercury's rocky surface is covered with impact marks.

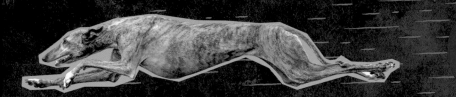

#25

True or False:

A greyhound

could beat a cheetah
in a long-distance race.

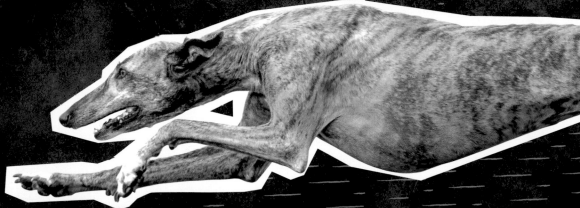

ANSWER: **True**

Winner!

ABLE TO REACH A TOP SPEED OF UP TO 70 MILES AN HOUR (113 KMH), cheetahs have the upper hand in a sprinting contest. But these big cats **can run for only a few hundred yards before they start to tire out.** Though they max out at only about half that speed, greyhounds can keep up their speed for an extended period of time. These long-legged canines are lean and light on their feet: When running, **they spend 75 percent of their time in the air.** No wonder they look like they're flying! Greyhounds also have large hearts and lungs. This makes them **efficient at moving oxygen through their bodies,** which also helps them run faster than other breeds.

#26

True or False:

Babies **blink** more than adults.

59

ANSWER: **False**

ADULTS BLINK ABOUT 15 TIMES A MINUTE, WHILE BABIES BLINK ONLY ONCE OR TWICE A MINUTE. Scientists think this could be because **babies are trying to soak up as much of what they see as possible.** Blinking is important because **it keeps our eyes safe from dust and prevents them from drying out.** When we blink, we spread salty fluids from the tear glands around our eyes and renew tear film, a smooth, moist layer covering our eyeballs.

Instant Genius
Most people can't sneeze with their eyes open.

How old was a #27 baby woolly mammoth discovered in 2007?

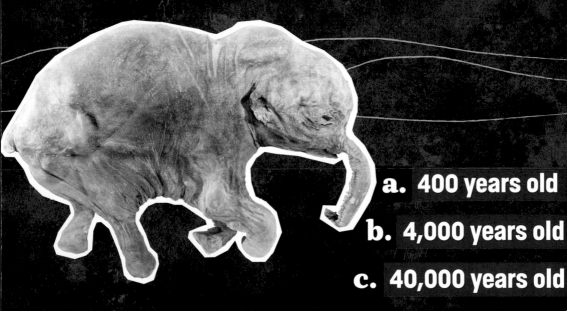

a. 400 years old

b. 4,000 years old

c. 40,000 years old

ANSWER: C

40,000 years old

WOOLLY MAMMOTHS WERE ELEPHANT-LIKE MAMMALS THAT LIVED FROM ABOUT 400,000 YEARS AGO TO ABOUT 10,000 YEARS AGO. Roughly the size of today's elephants, mammoths were **covered with shaggy dark brown hair** and had long, curved tusks. We know a lot about them thanks to Lyuba, a frozen baby mammoth discovered in Siberia in 2007. **Lyuba still had her baby teeth, which helped scientists determine her age.** She also had mud in her lungs, which led scientists to believe she fell into a lake while drinking water. Thanks to the Siberia's freezing temperatures and the mud, Lyuba's body was preserved perfectly and protected from scavengers.

Which is the hottest?

#28

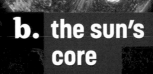

b. **the sun's core**

a. **lava**

c. **lightning**

NOW YOU KNOW!
It would take about a year and a half to drive across the sun. This might make it seem like the sun is huge, but there are other stars that are 100 times bigger!

ANSWER: **b** the sun's core

Instant Genius
The sun is the hottest object in the solar system.

LAVA, WHICH IS MOLTEN ROCK THAT FLOWS FROM A VOLCANO, CAN REACH TEMPERATURES OF MORE THAN 2,000°F (1,090°C). When lightning strikes, **it can heat the air it passes through to 50,000°F (27,800°C)**—five times hotter than the surface of the sun. **But neither of those compare to the sun's core,** where the sun's energy is created. **Here, it's 27,000,000°F (15,000,000°C)!** Energy from the core makes its way to the surface of the sun. It then leaves the sun and reaches Earth as light.

How long does it take your body to **fully digest food?**

a. **45 minutes**

b. **24 hours**

c. **2 to 5 days**

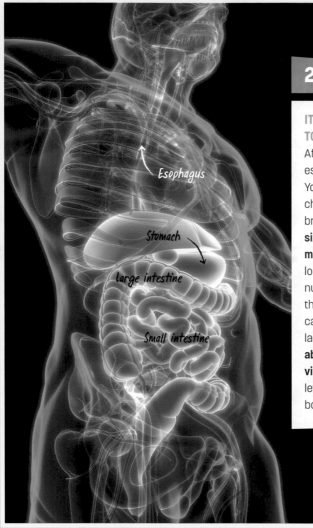

Esophagus

Stomach

Large intestine

Small intestine

2 to 5 days

IT TAKES ANYWHERE FROM TWO TO FIVE DAYS TO DIGEST FOOD. After you eat, food travels down your esophagus and into your stomach. Your stomach then produces special chemicals, called enzymes, that break down the food. **After two to six hours in your stomach, the food moves to your small intestine,** a long tube that absorbs the food's nutrients and minerals. At this point, the food is a soft mush. The mush, called chyme, then moves on to your large intestine. **Your large intestine absorbs any remaining water, vitamins, and minerals.** Anything left after that is eliminated from our bodies a few days later.

Instant Genius

The adult digestive system is about 30 feet (9 m) long.

Raspberries

#30

are part of which plant family?

a. the rose family

b. the orange family

c. the tomato family

ANSWER: **a**

the rose family

THE ROSE FAMILY ALSO INCLUDES APPLES, PEARS, ALMONDS, PEACHES, APRICOTS, PLUMS, CHERRIES, STRAWBERRIES, AND BLACKBERRIES, as well as flowers with thorny stems. Flowering plants from this family have a cuplike shape with five petals and oval leaves. **Each raspberry is not a single berry but rather a cluster of 100 tiny fruits.** There are 200 varieties of raspberries, which **can be red, black, purple, yellow, and even blue.** The states of Washington, Oregon, and California grow the most raspberries in the United States.

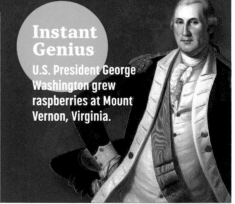

Instant Genius

U.S. President George Washington grew raspberries at Mount Vernon, Virginia.

Bombardier beetles

#31

have what extraordinary ability?

a. They can hold their breath for more than an hour.

b. They can eat a mouse in one bite.

c. They can shoot poison out of their bottoms 500 times a second.

Watch this!

They can shoot poison out of their bottoms 500 times a second.

BOMBARDIER BEETLES ARE FOUND ON EVERY CONTINENT EXCEPT ANTARCTICA. What makes this beetle unique is its defense mechanism against predators such as spiders, birds, and insects. **The abdomen of a bombardier beetle contains chambers that separately store two chemical weapons: hydroquinone and hydrogen peroxide.** When the beetle senses danger, these two chemicals combine, giving off **heat intense enough to bring the mixture almost to a boiling point.** Then, *bam!* The beetle shoots the burning, toxic, stinky spray out of its rear end with a loud popping sound.

Instant Genius

The spray of a bombardier beetle can make a frog vomit.

What is the only bird that can fly backward?

#32

b. the bald eagle

a. the hummingbird

c. the cardinal

NOW YOU KNOW!
Some hummingbirds can beat their wings 200 times per second. A hummingbird's heart can beat more than 1,200 times per minute!

ANSWER: a

the hummingbird

HUMMINGBIRDS ARE THE ONLY BIRDS THAT CAN FLY BACKWARD. This special ability has to do with their wing structure—a unique ball-and-socket joint at the shoulder that allows their wings to perform a 180-degree rotation. **Hummingbirds can move their wings up, down, backward, forward, and even in a figure-eight motion.** On the ground, however, hummingbirds are not as nimble. **They can't walk or hop.** Their tiny legs can move only sideways while they're perched.

Instant Genius
The Cuban bee hummingbird weighs less than a penny.

33

True or False:

The youngest person to **sail solo** around the world was 18 years old.

ANSWER: False

CIRCUMNAVIGATING (SAILING AROUND) THE GLOBE IS AN AMAZING ACCOMPLISHMENT. But when you're a teenager doing it alone—on a sailboat—it's even more impressive! **Dutch sailor Laura Dekker was only 14** when she set out to become the youngest person to sail around the world by herself. She spent **almost two years at sea on a 38-foot (11.6 m) sailboat named** *Guppy*. By the time she completed her trip, she was 16. You could say that Dekker has sailing in her blood: She was born during a seven-year sailing trip that her parents were taking. There have been five teenagers who have sailed solo around the world. Dekker is the youngest.

NOW YOU KNOW!
A man named Joshua Slocum was the first person to sail around the world alone. He spent his life at sea starting at age 16 and never left the open waters.

Why do dogs hate thunderstorms?

a. They don't like the sound of thunder.

b. They don't like the brightness of lightning.

c. They don't like getting their fur wet.

Tell me when it's over.

ANSWER: a

They don't like the sound of thunder.

DOGS FEAR LOUD NOISES, SO MANY OF THEM ARE SCARED WHEN THUNDER BOOMS. Some dogs can even tell when a storm is brewing! Just like people, dogs can see a darkening sky and feel the wind pick up. But dogs have another way to sense when wild weather is on the way. Before a storm, there is a decrease in air pressure, which is the weight of the air that is pushing down on us. **Dogs can pick up on this change** and might associate it with thunder. This may upset dogs as much as the noise itself! To help them cope with rumbling thunder, **dogs can wear a special vest** that puts gentle pressure around their torso—like a calming hug.

How long can an astronaut's footprints last on the moon?

#35

a. one day

b. one year

c. up to one million years

ANSWER: C

up to one million years

ON JULY 20, 1969, NEIL ARMSTRONG WALKED ON THE MOON. His footprint was the first human footprint placed there, and it's still on the rocky surface. Why? **There is no atmosphere and therefore no wind to blow it away.** But there is something that could erase the footprints: moonquakes. During the Apollo missions to the moon, astronauts placed four quake detectors on the moon's surface. **They picked up at least four different types of moonquakes:** Deep quakes hundreds of miles below the surface, shallow quakes below the surface, vibrations of hits from meteorites, and quakes caused when the sun heats up the moon's icy crust.

The area where Neil Armstrong first walked on the moon

Instant Genius

Unlike earthquakes, which last only a few minutes, moonquakes can go on for a few hours.

You drink the **same** water as *T. rex* did millions of years ago.

#36

ANSWER: True

YES, IT'S TRUE! HOW IS THIS POSSIBLE? THE ANSWER IS EARTH'S WATER CYCLE. Liquid water is found in oceans, rivers, lakes—and even underground. Solid water, or ice, is found in glaciers, snow, and ice sheets at the North and South Poles. **Water vapor—a gas—is found everywhere on Earth, including in the atmosphere.** During the water cycle, heat from the sun causes liquid water droplets to evaporate into the air, turning into water vapor. In the air, the **vapor cools and condenses, turning back into liquid.** This is how clouds form. When a cloud is full of water, the water begins to fall back to Earth as rain, snow, sleet, or hail. **Then the cycle repeats.**

Instant Genius

Only 3 percent of the water on Earth is fresh water

How much does it
cost to make a

#37 penny?

a. exactly one penny

b. more than a penny

c. less than a penny

ANSWER: b

more than a penny

THE UNITED STATES DEPARTMENT OF THE TREASURY IS A NATIONAL AGENCY THAT MANAGES THE FEDERAL GOVERNMENT'S MONEY, including collecting taxes and creating currency. Currency is money, and it includes both coins and bills. Within the Department of the Treasury, there are two divisions that actually create money. The U.S. Bureau of Engraving and Printing makes paper bills, and the U.S. Mint makes coins. Coins are made out of metals. **The cost of making a penny depends on how much the metals it's made from—**copper and zinc—cost at the time the penny is made. For years, it has cost more to make and ship pennies than what they are actually worth.

Instant Genius

In 2021, it costs almost two pennies to make one penny.

What's more **lethal,** a shark or a chair?

#38

ANSWER: **a chair**

THOUGH SHARK ATTACKS DO HAPPEN, THEY ARE RARE: In 2020, there were **less than 60 shark attacks worldwide.** Sharks show little interest in eating people; humans are not part of their natural diet. The only reason one might attack is if it mistakes a person for a fish or marine mammal, such as a seal. Falls involving chairs, on the other hand, account for **hundreds of deaths per year.**

This is life-size!

Instant Genius

Sharks are born with their teeth to help protect themselves.

#39

How long does an **eyelash** last?

a. about four to five weeks

b. about six to eight weeks

c. about one year

85

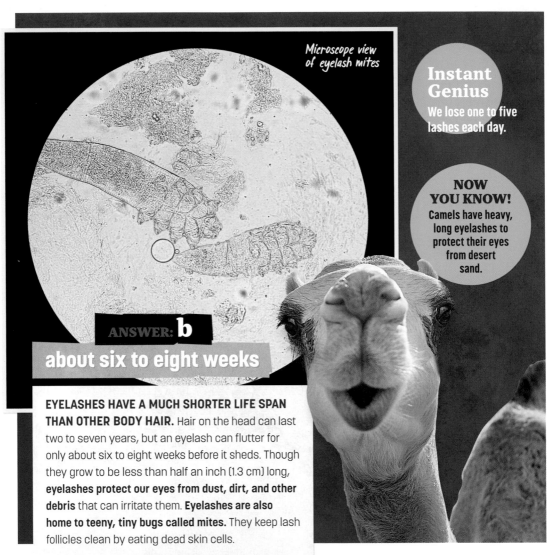

Microscope view of eyelash mites

Instant Genius
We lose one to five lashes each day.

NOW YOU KNOW!
Camels have heavy, long eyelashes to protect their eyes from desert sand.

ANSWER: **b**

about six to eight weeks

EYELASHES HAVE A MUCH SHORTER LIFE SPAN THAN OTHER BODY HAIR. Hair on the head can last two to seven years, but an eyelash can flutter for only about six to eight weeks before it sheds. Though they grow to be less than half an inch (1.3 cm) long, **eyelashes protect our eyes from dust, dirt, and other debris** that can irritate them. **Eyelashes are also home to teeny, tiny bugs called mites.** They keep lash follicles clean by eating dead skin cells.

How many species of
gorilla
are there?

#40

Great question!

a. 2 species

b. 5 species

c. 7 species

Eastern gorilla

Western gorillas

2 species

GORILLAS ARE LARGE APES THAT ARE CLOSELY RELATED TO HUMANS. There are two main species of gorillas: **The eastern Gorilla** and the **western Gorilla.** Both species live in the tropical rainforests of Central Africa. **Gorillas are intelligent, social animals.** They live in family groups of up to 50 and have been seen making and using tools. In fact, one female gorilla was seen using a stick to test the depth of water in a pond before walking in. She kept poking the stick into the water as she walked to make sure it was shallow!

Instant Genius
Gorillas sleep in nests made of leaves and branches.

How many
lightning bolts
strike
Earth each day?

#41

a. **80**   b. **800**   c. **more than 8,000,000**

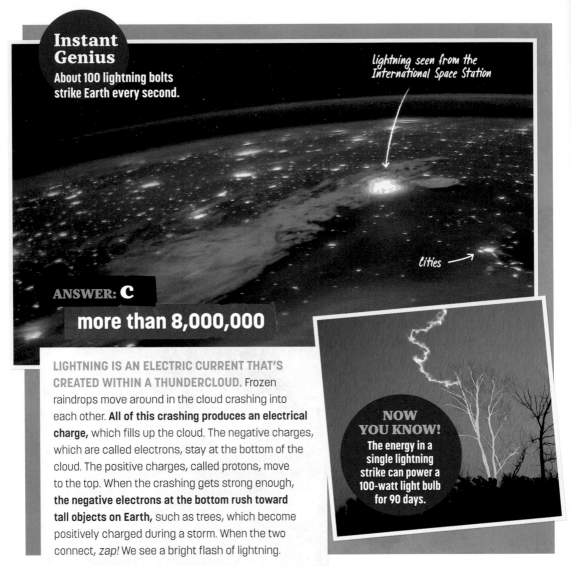

Lightning seen from the International Space Station

Cities →

ANSWER: C

more than 8,000,000

LIGHTNING IS AN ELECTRIC CURRENT THAT'S CREATED WITHIN A THUNDERCLOUD. Frozen raindrops move around in the cloud crashing into each other. **All of this crashing produces an electrical charge,** which fills up the cloud. The negative charges, which are called electrons, stay at the bottom of the cloud. The positive charges, called protons, move to the top. When the crashing gets strong enough, **the negative electrons at the bottom rush toward tall objects on Earth,** such as trees, which become positively charged during a storm. When the two connect, *zap!* We see a bright flash of lightning.

NOW YOU KNOW!

The energy in a single lightning strike can power a 100-watt light bulb for 90 days.

The man who invented the Pringles potato chip can was **buried in one.**

#42

ANSWER: **True**

WHEN POTATO CHIPS WERE FIRST INVENTED, THEY WERE AVAILABLE ONLY IN RESTAURANTS. Then, in 1926, a woman in California had the idea of **packaging the chips in bags to keep them fresh.** Eventually, the bags were puffed with air to better protect the chips, but chips can still be crushed. **Then, in 1968, along came Pringles, the first canned potato chips.** The inventor, Fredric Baur, was so proud of his packaging that he asked for some of his ashes be buried in it. When the 89-year-old died, **his family stopped at a store on the way to the funeral home to buy a can of Pringles** to hold their father's ashes.

Instant Genius

Potato chips are America's number one snack food.

Why do scientists think it's possible that life exists on

Mars?

a. They found oxygen.

b. They found water.

c. They found food.

North pole

South pole

ANSWER: b | **They found water.**

FOR CENTURIES, SCIENTISTS HAVE WONDERED IF LIFE EXISTS ON MARS—our neighbor and the fourth planet from the sun. One of the biggest clues that it might is the presence of water there. **Life as we know it can't exist without water.** Though Mars has a thin atmosphere that does not allow water to flow or remain on the surface, scientists have determined that **there is ice at its poles.** There is also evidence of a large saltwater lake under the planet's southern polar ice cap. Using radar, scientists have discovered three other lakes on the red planet, too. If water does exist, it's very possible life does also.

Instant Genius

Sunsets on Mars are blue.

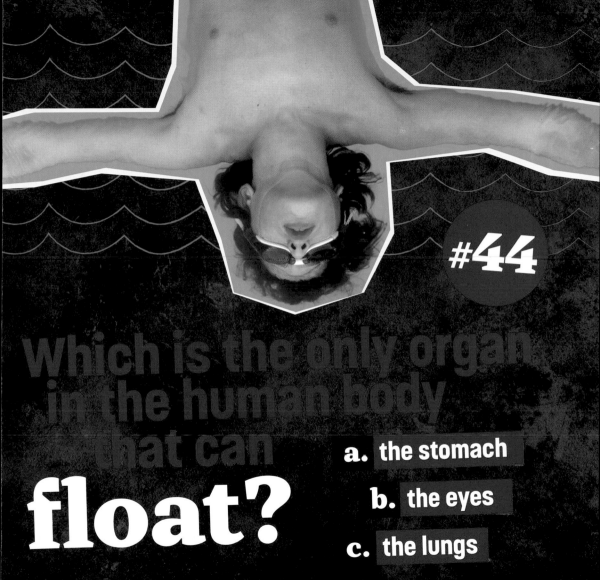

#44

Which is the only organ in the human body that can **float?**

a. the stomach

b. the eyes

c. the lungs

95

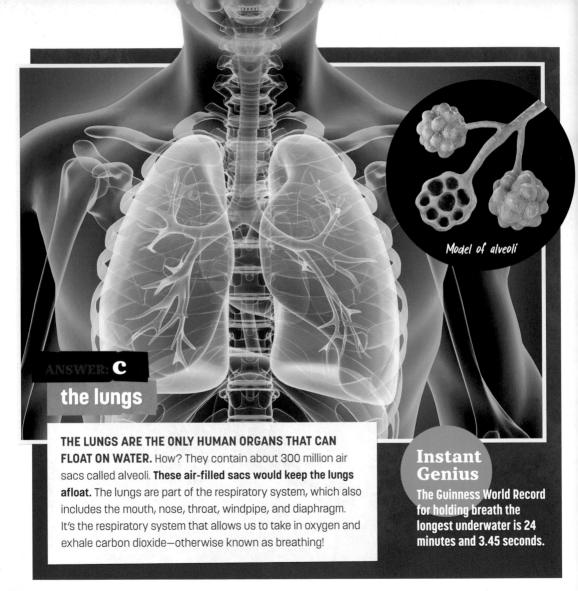

Model of alveoli

ANSWER: c

the lungs

THE LUNGS ARE THE ONLY HUMAN ORGANS THAT CAN FLOAT ON WATER. How? They contain about 300 million air sacs called alveoli. **These air-filled sacs would keep the lungs afloat.** The lungs are part of the respiratory system, which also includes the mouth, nose, throat, windpipe, and diaphragm. It's the respiratory system that allows us to take in oxygen and exhale carbon dioxide—otherwise known as breathing!

Instant Genius

The Guinness World Record for holding breath the longest underwater is 24 minutes and 3.45 seconds.

#45

True or False:

The sun is a
star.

THE SUN IS A KIND OF STAR KNOWN AS A YELLOW DWARF. Though it's much, much larger than Earth, the sun is actually considered **a medium-size star.** Stars produce their own energy through a reaction of gases. The sun produces its energy by converting helium gas into hydrogen gas. This conversion creates huge amounts of energy that reach Earth as the **heat and light all living things need to survive.** The sun is also the largest body in our solar system. Its gravity holds the solar system together, keeping everything from the largest planets to the smallest particles of dust within its orbit.

NOW YOU KNOW!
It takes about 8 minutes and 20 seconds for the sun's light to reach our planet. It takes about 3 minutes for the sun's light to reach Mercury.

Instant Genius
More than 1 million Earths could fit inside the sun.

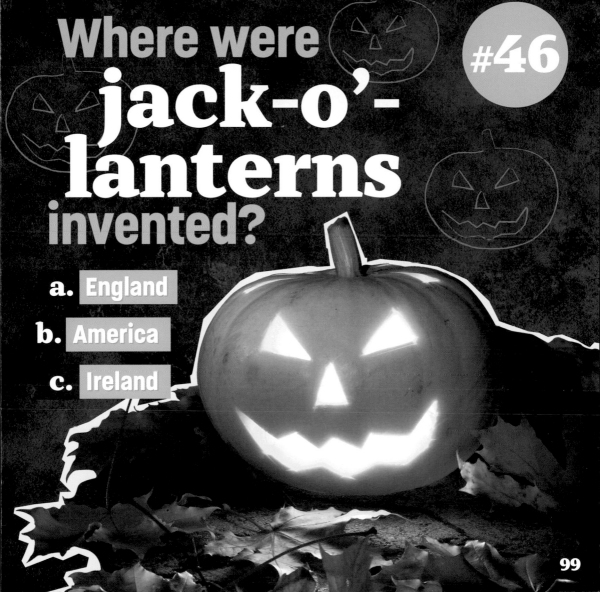

Where were jack-o'-lanterns invented?

#46

a. England

b. America

c. Ireland

ANSWER: C **Ireland**

CARVING PUMPKINS INTO JACK-O'-LANTERNS IS A POPULAR HALLOWEEN TRADITION THAT BEGAN HUNDREDS OF YEARS AGO IN IRELAND. Back then, Irish people carved scary faces into **turnips, potatoes, and even large beets** to keep away evil spirits. When Irish immigrants came to America, they switched to pumpkins, which were larger and easier to carve, and **a new Halloween tradition was born.** Now pumpkins are commonly placed on stoops in the fall and carved before Halloween night.

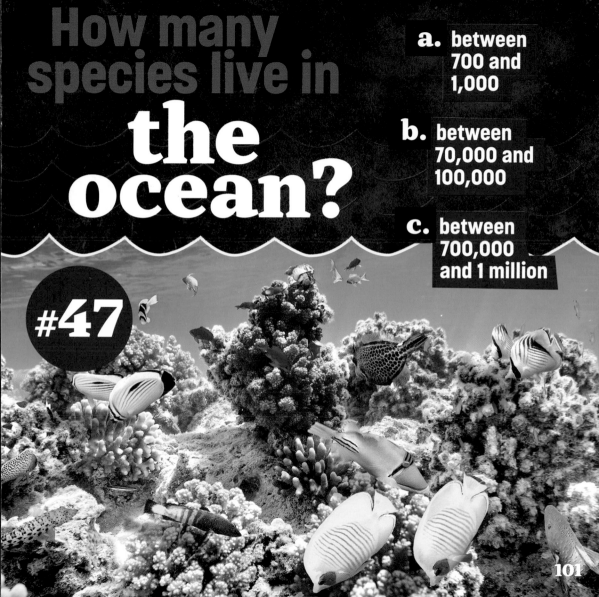

How many species live in the ocean?

a. between 700 and 1,000

b. between 70,000 and 100,000

c. between 700,000 and 1 million

#47

101

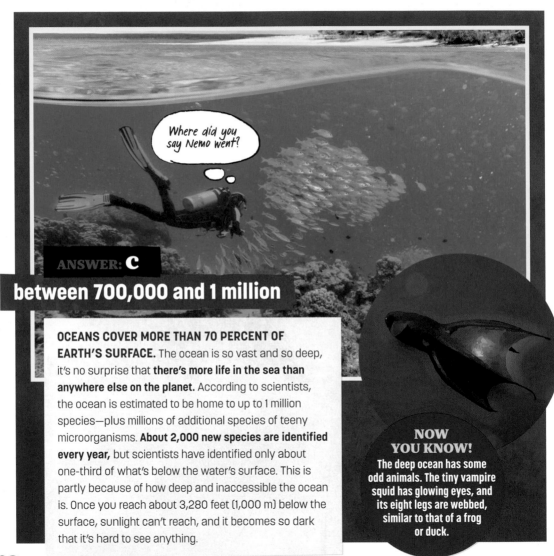

Where did you say Nemo went?

ANSWER: C

between 700,000 and 1 million

OCEANS COVER MORE THAN 70 PERCENT OF EARTH'S SURFACE. The ocean is so vast and so deep, it's no surprise that **there's more life in the sea than anywhere else on the planet.** According to scientists, the ocean is estimated to be home to up to 1 million species—plus millions of additional species of teeny microorganisms. **About 2,000 new species are identified every year,** but scientists have identified only about one-third of what's below the water's surface. This is partly because of how deep and inaccessible the ocean is. Once you reach about 3,280 feet (1,000 m) below the surface, sunlight can't reach, and it becomes so dark that it's hard to see anything.

NOW YOU KNOW!
The deep ocean has some odd animals. The tiny vampire squid has glowing eyes, and its eight legs are webbed, similar to that of a frog or duck.

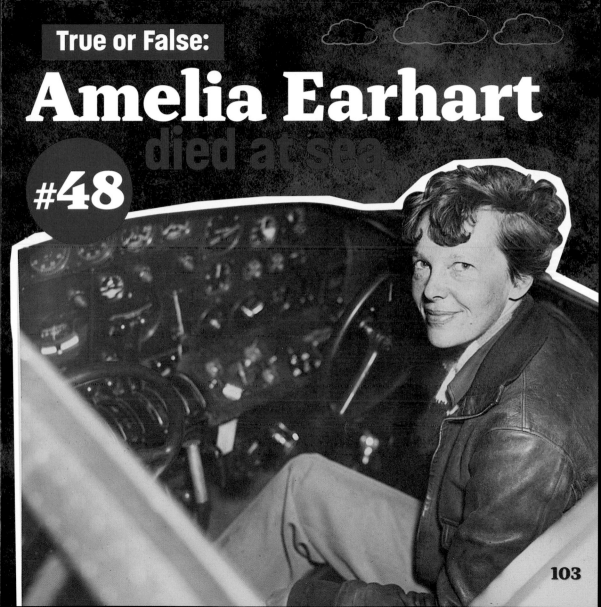

True or False:

Amelia Earhart

died at sea

#48

103

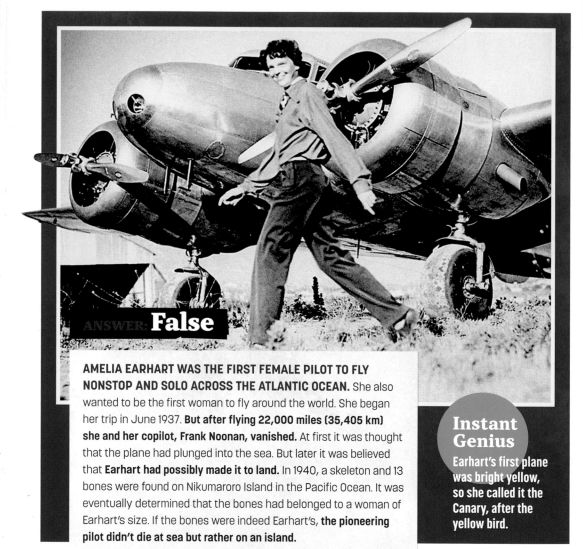

ANSWER: **False**

AMELIA EARHART WAS THE FIRST FEMALE PILOT TO FLY NONSTOP AND SOLO ACROSS THE ATLANTIC OCEAN. She also wanted to be the first woman to fly around the world. She began her trip in June 1937. **But after flying 22,000 miles (35,405 km) she and her copilot, Frank Noonan, vanished.** At first it was thought that the plane had plunged into the sea. But later it was believed that **Earhart had possibly made it to land.** In 1940, a skeleton and 13 bones were found on Nikumaroro Island in the Pacific Ocean. It was eventually determined that the bones had belonged to a woman of Earhart's size. If the bones were indeed Earhart's, **the pioneering pilot didn't die at sea but rather on an island.**

Instant Genius

Earhart's first plane was bright yellow, so she called it the Canary, after the yellow bird.

What's the **fastest creature** in the animal world?

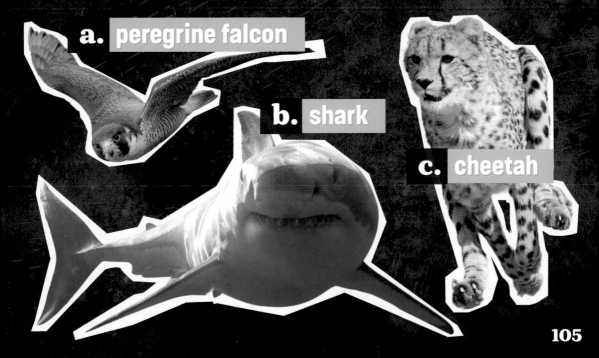

a. **peregrine falcon**

b. **shark**

c. **cheetah**

peregrine falcon

THE PEREGRINE FALCON IS NOT ONLY THE FASTEST BIRD BUT ALSO THE FASTEST MEMBER OF THE ANIMAL WORLD. It can dive into water at speeds of **200 miles an hour (322 kmh).** It does this to catch fish to eat. The super flier's speed is thanks to its very large keel, a ridge on its breastbone where its muscles attach. The keel gives this bird extra muscle power for maximum speed. **The peregrine falcon also has a pointed, aerodynamic body** with stiff wings that sweep back, giving the bird a streamlined shape well suited for swooping on prey.

Instant Genius

Peregrines live on all continents except Antarctica.

NOW YOU KNOW!

Sailfish are considered by many scientists to be the fastest fish in the ocean. They can swim at speeds of up to about 70 miles an hour (113 kmh). That's faster than many cars travel on the highway!

Which is the only food that **never** goes bad?

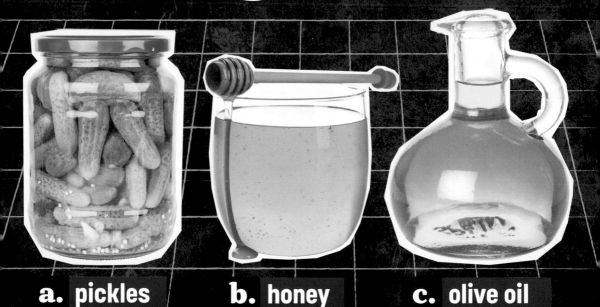

a. pickles   **b.** honey   **c.** olive oil

ANSWER: **b**

honey

HONEY IS RECOGNIZED AS THE ONLY FOOD THAT DOESN'T SPOIL. Archeologists found honey thousands of years old in **ancient Egyptian tombs, and it was still good to eat!** What's honey secret to a long life? Honey has a high sugar content, contains little water, and is extremely acidic. This combination **kills off any bacteria that could spoil it.** Honeybees make honey using nectar from flowers. A honeybee will visit 50 to 100 flowers on one trip out of the hive. To make one pound (0.5 kg) of honey, the bees in a colony must visit **2 million flowers and fly more than 55,000 miles (88,514 km).**

Instant Genius
Honey has been used in medicine for more than 5,000 years.

True or False:

#51

Cats purr only when they are happy.

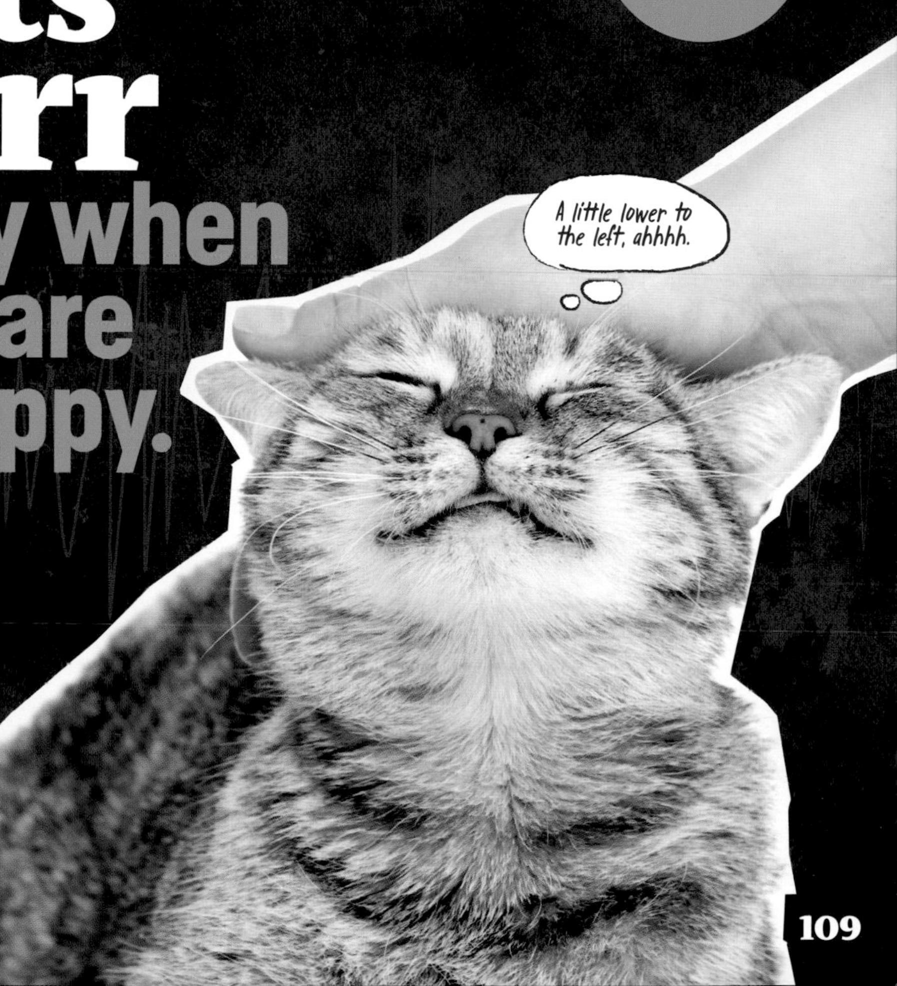

ANSWER: **False**

CATS PURR SOFTLY, AND THEY DO SO TO COMMUNICATE WITH THOSE CLOSE TO THEM.
A mother cat will purr to let her newborn kittens, who are born deaf and blind, know she's there. **Sometimes cats purr to signal distress**—when they are scared, hungry, or hurt. But mostly cats purr when they are happy and content, such as **when kittens are drinking mom's milk** or cats are grooming, relaxing, or being friendly.

Instant Genius
A cat might chirp when it's excited or to say hello.

NOW YOU KNOW!
Merlin, a black and white cat from England, holds the record for the loudest purr. His purr is more than twice as loud as the average cat and sounds like a bathroom shower!

What is **unique** to every person?

#52

a. their fingerprints

b. their tongue print

c. their fingerprints and tongue print

111

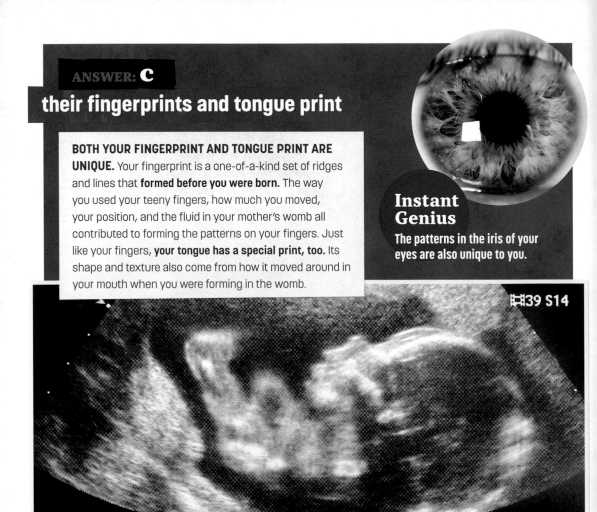

their fingerprints and tongue print

BOTH YOUR FINGERPRINT AND TONGUE PRINT ARE UNIQUE. Your fingerprint is a one-of-a-kind set of ridges and lines that **formed before you were born.** The way you used your teeny fingers, how much you moved, your position, and the fluid in your mother's womb all contributed to forming the patterns on your fingers. Just like your fingers, **your tongue has a special print, too.** Its shape and texture also come from how it moved around in your mouth when you were forming in the womb.

Instant Genius

The patterns in the iris of your eyes are also unique to you.

⊞39 S14

Ultrasound scan of baby in womb

112

Hermit crabs
got their name because they prefer to live alone.

#53

The more the merrier.

ANSWER: False

NOW YOU KNOW!
Hermit crabs are not true crabs. Unlike the blue crab, for example, a hermit crab does not have a hard exoskeleton and can't grow its own shells.

A HERMIT CRAB IS A SMALL CREATURE THAT USES ANOTHER ANIMAL'S SHELL TO MAKE ITS HOME AND PROTECT ITS SOFT BODY. The word "hermit" refers to someone who prefers to live alone, but **hermit crabs are actually social creatures.** In the wild, they live together in colonies. Being part of a group works out well because when one crab grows too big for its shell and sheds it, there is another crab waiting to move in! In their natural habitat, **hermit crabs can live for up to 30 years,** growing larger and larger and moving into bigger and bigger shells.

Instant Genius
There are more than 800 species of hermit crabs.

How deep is the deepest part of the ocean?

#54

Wow, that's deep.

a. less than 1 mile (1.6 km)

b. nearly 3 miles (4.8 km)

c. nearly 7 miles (11.3 km)

nearly 7 miles (11.3 km)

IMAGINE A GASH IN EARTH'S CRUST FIVE TIMES LONGER THAN THE GRAND CANYON AND MUCH MORE CAVERNOUS. Well, it exists in the **Pacific Ocean, between Guam and the Philippines.** At the deepest point of the **Mariana Trench,** there is a section called Challenger Deep that goes nearly **7 miles (11.3 km) down.** It descends so far that if you plunged Mount Everest into this pitch-black hole, the mountain's tip wouldn't even clear the surface of the ocean.

Mariana Trench

Challenger Deep

NOW YOU KNOW!

Challenger Deep got its name from a British Royal Navy ship called the *Challenger*, which traveled around the world gathering information about the oceans.

True or False:

A banana peel

can be used to
clean your hands
and shine
your shoes.

#55

117

ANSWER: True

TURNS OUT THE SLIMY SKIN WE TOSS WHENEVER WE EAT A BANANA IS ACTUALLY PRETTY USEFUL. It can be used to remove ink stains from your hands. How? **The oils in the peel can help lift the stains.** Bananas are loaded with potassium, which is also the key ingredient to restoring shine to your shoes. This mineral absorbs well into leather. All you have to do is **buff your shoes with the inside of the peel** and wipe your shoes with a clean cloth. Scuffs should disappear.

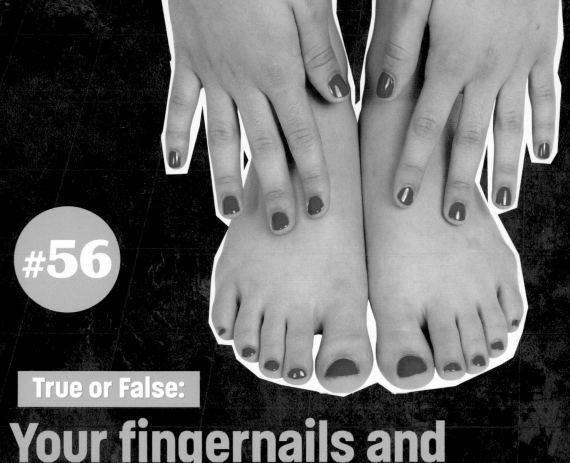

#56

True or False:

Your fingernails and toenails grow at the same rate.

Instant Genius

Fingernails and toenails grow faster in the summertime.

ANSWER: False

FINGERNAILS GROW ABOUT FOUR TIMES FASTER THAN TOENAILS. Made of a protein called **keratin (the same stuff hair is made of),** nails protect the tips of the fingers and toes and make it possible to scratch or do things like pluck leaves from your clothes. **Fingernails grow about one-tenth of an inch each month**—a bit more than the thickness of a nickel—and it can take about three to six months to replace a nail.

NOW YOU KNOW!

The Guinness World Record holder for the person with the longest fingernails finally cut them off. Altogether, their length was equivalent to a London bus.

True or False:

Butterflies
taste with their
feet.

#57

121

ANSWER: **True**

TO FEED, A BUTTERFLY UNWINDS A LONG, SKINNY PART OF ITS BODY CALLED A PROBOSCIS and uses it like a straw to suck up fluids such as flower nectar and fruit juice. A butterfly will sometimes also sip from a mud puddle to absorb minerals. Once it is finished drinking, its proboscis coils back up. **To taste, butterflies rely on sensors on their feet.** A female will stand on a leaf and taste it to see if it's safe for her caterpillars to eat. If it is, she will lay her eggs on it.

Instant Genius
Butterflies don't have two wings; they actually have four.

What produces most of Earth's oxygen?

#58

a. the oceans   b. trees   c. grass

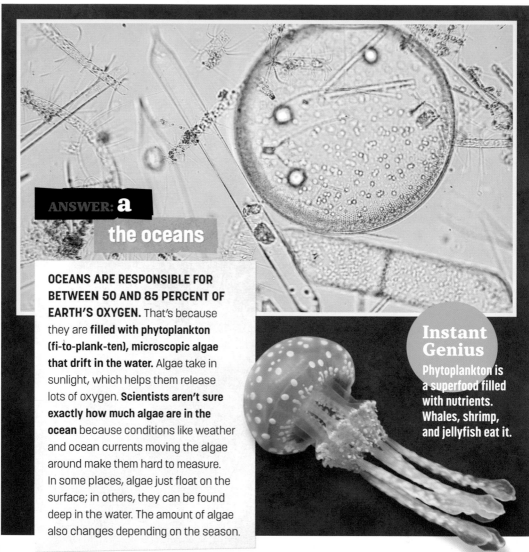

ANSWER: a

the oceans

OCEANS ARE RESPONSIBLE FOR BETWEEN 50 AND 85 PERCENT OF EARTH'S OXYGEN. That's because they are **filled with phytoplankton (fi-to-plank-ten), microscopic algae that drift in the water.** Algae take in sunlight, which helps them release lots of oxygen. **Scientists aren't sure exactly how much algae are in the ocean** because conditions like weather and ocean currents moving the algae around make them hard to measure. In some places, algae just float on the surface; in others, they can be found deep in the water. The amount of algae also changes depending on the season.

Instant Genius
Phytoplankton is a superfood filled with nutrients. Whales, shrimp, and jellyfish eat it.

The **London Bridge** that kept falling down is now located in Scotland.

#59

125

London Bridge, Arizona

ANSWER: **False**

LONDON BRIDGE WAS ORIGINALLY BUILT IN THE 1830S OVER THE RIVER THAMES IN LONDON. Years later, when people started driving cars, the bridge started sinking into the ground because it couldn't handle the weight of the vehicles. Officials in London knew that the bridge would need to be replaced. **In 1968, an American businessman bought the bridge for more than $2 million.** Pieces of the bridge were taken apart and **shipped to the U.S. state of Arizona,** where it was rebuilt in the desert in the hope of attracting tourists to the area. At first, the bridge sat over land. Later a canal was dug underneath and filled with water. The relocated London Bridge eventually did become a tourist attraction!

How many gallons of
blood
does the human
heart circulate
through the
body per day?

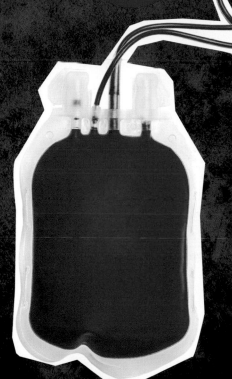

a. about 1.5 gallons (5.7 L)

b. about 5.5 gallons (20.8 L)

c. about 8.5 gallons (32.2 L)

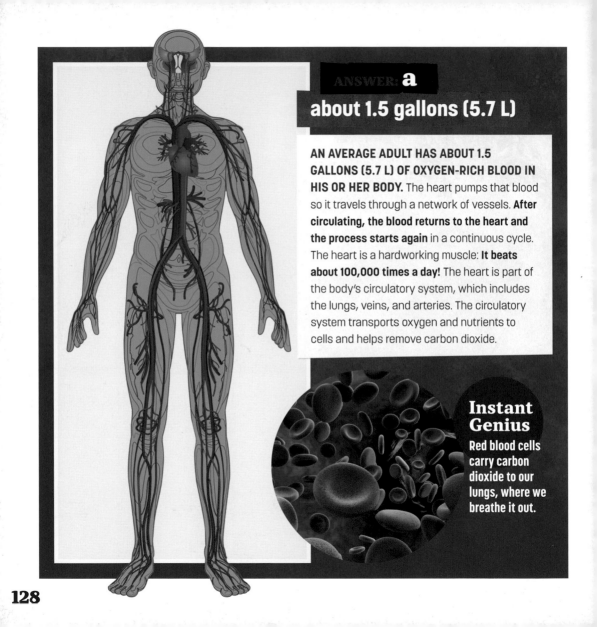

about 1.5 gallons (5.7 L)

AN AVERAGE ADULT HAS ABOUT 1.5 GALLONS (5.7 L) OF OXYGEN-RICH BLOOD IN HIS OR HER BODY. The heart pumps that blood so it travels through a network of vessels. **After circulating, the blood returns to the heart and the process starts again** in a continuous cycle. The heart is a hardworking muscle: **It beats about 100,000 times a day!** The heart is part of the body's circulatory system, which includes the lungs, veins, and arteries. The circulatory system transports oxygen and nutrients to cells and helps remove carbon dioxide.

Instant Genius
Red blood cells carry carbon dioxide to our lungs, where we breathe it out.

What is the heaviest animal of all time?

a. African bush elephant

b. blue whale

c. hippo

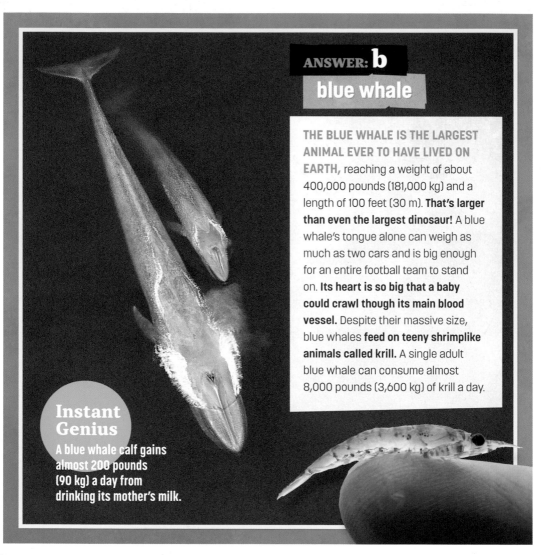

blue whale

THE BLUE WHALE IS THE LARGEST ANIMAL EVER TO HAVE LIVED ON EARTH, reaching a weight of about 400,000 pounds (181,000 kg) and a length of 100 feet (30 m). **That's larger than even the largest dinosaur!** A blue whale's tongue alone can weigh as much as two cars and is big enough for an entire football team to stand on. **Its heart is so big that a baby could crawl though its main blood vessel.** Despite their massive size, blue whales **feed on teeny shrimplike animals called krill.** A single adult blue whale can consume almost 8,000 pounds (3,600 kg) of krill a day.

Instant Genius

A blue whale calf gains almost 200 pounds (90 kg) a day from drinking its mother's milk.

True or False:

Your ears and nose
never stop
growing.

#62

l'mon, really?

Smells fishy
to me.

131

ANSWER: True

WE GROW WHEN THE CELLS IN OUR BODIES DUPLICATE.
Most people stop growing taller at about 18 years old, but
our ears and noses continue to grow throughout life, just
at a slower pace. **Noses and ears are made of a soft, bendy
tissue called cartilage,** which is also found in our joints and
throat. Cartilage helps connect bones, keeps joints flexible,
and cushions bones against impact—and it keeps growing
throughout our lives. As humans age, **gravity begins to
break down cartilage.** This can cause earlobes to sag and
appear as though they are growing longer.

Instant Genius
A shark doesn't have bones. Its
skeleton is made of cartilage.

If you played the
saxophone in space, how would it sound?

#63

a. **silent**

b. **squeaky**

c. **symphonic**

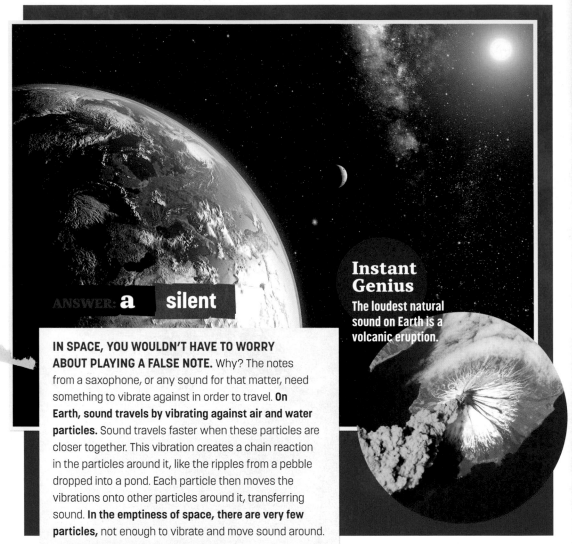

ANSWER: **a** **silent**

Instant Genius

The loudest natural sound on Earth is a volcanic eruption.

IN SPACE, YOU WOULDN'T HAVE TO WORRY ABOUT PLAYING A FALSE NOTE. Why? The notes from a saxophone, or any sound for that matter, need something to vibrate against in order to travel. **On Earth, sound travels by vibrating against air and water particles.** Sound travels faster when these particles are closer together. This vibration creates a chain reaction in the particles around it, like the ripples from a pebble dropped into a pond. Each particle then moves the vibrations onto other particles around it, transferring sound. **In the emptiness of space, there are very few particles,** not enough to vibrate and move sound around.

Where is the town with the **longest name** in the world located?

#64

a. Germany

b. England

c. New Zealand

135

ANSWER: C

New Zealand

IT'S TAUMATAWHAKATANGIHANGAKOAUAUOTA-MATEATURIPUKAKAPIKIMAUNGAHORONUKUPO-KAIWHENUAKITANATAHU. This small hill town in New Zealand has **85 letters in its name!** In English, the name translates to "the place where Tamatea, the man with the big knees, who slid, climbed, and swallowed mountains, known as 'landeater,' played his flute to his loved one." **To locals, it's simply Taumata Hill.** The name comes from the Maori, the first people to live on the islands of New Zealand. According to Maori legend, **Tamatea was a great traveler who came to New Zealand from Maui, Hawaii,** in a canoe with his pet alligator, serpent, and dog.

Instant Genius

Å is a tiny fishing village in Norway, and Y is a village in France.

136

A rainbow
is always in the shape of an arc.

#65

137

ANSWER: False

WHEN WE SEE A RAINBOW IN THE SKY, IT LOOKS LIKE AN ARC, OR A CURVED LINE. But that curved line actually continues into a full circle. **We just can't see the bottom of the circle because the ground gets in the way.** A rainbow is a reflection of the sun's light, which appears white but is made up of a spectrum of colors. Sunlight travels through space in the form of wavelengths. When it passes through raindrops, the raindrops bend the wavelengths, which separates the sunlight into the different colors.

NOW YOU KNOW!

The colors of a rainbow are red, orange, yellow, green, blue, indigo, and violet, also known as ROY G. BIV.

True or False:

The **most stolen** food in the world is cheese.

#66

139

ANSWER: True

AT LEAST 4 PERCENT OF CHEESE DISAPPEARS FROM STORE SHELVES ALL OVER THE WORLD. But why do thieves resort to stealing cheese? According to criminologists (scientists who study crimes), cheese is a popular food to steal because it's kept in a grocery store's refrigerated sections, which have **fewer surveillance cameras** than its shelves, and because it's easy to hide. **Criminals resell the stolen cheese to restaurants and markets.**

Instant Genius

Milk from reindeer, llamas, yaks, and buffaloes has been made into cheese.

How many types of **bacteria** live in a dog's mouth?

#67

a. 600

b. 800

c. 1,000

141

ANSWER: a   600

EXPERTS HAVE FOUND THAT DOGS HAVE 600 TYPES OF BACTERIA IN THEIR MOUTHS. Where did all these bacteria come from? Well, dogs explore their world with their mouths and noses, so **a lot of the bacteria in their mouths come from all the sniffing and licking they do**— including their behinds and those of their other four-legged friends. To keep a dog's mouth healthy, **dogs should have their teeth brushed from the time they are puppies.**

Escherichia coli bacteria

#68

The
shape
of Earth
is a
perfect
sphere.

143

ANSWER: False

USING SATELLITES, SCIENTISTS CAN MEASURE EARTH'S SIZE AND SHAPE. Though it may look like a perfect sphere, it's not. In fact, **it bulges out in the middle!** In the 17th century, physicist **Sir Isaac Newton was the first scientist to propose that Earth was not perfectly round**. Newton suggested that our planet was squashed at its poles and swollen at the equator. He was correct. **Earth is squashed because of the force caused when it rotates.**

Venus

Mercury

Instant Genius

Mercury and Venus are the roundest planets. They are shaped almost like marbles.

True or False:

Yawns

are contagious.

#69

145

SCIENTISTS HAVE FOUND THAT YAWNS ARE CONTAGIOUS. According to one study, **if someone in a group yawns, more than half of the group will yawn, too.** A yawn is a reflex. When we yawn, the unconscious brain and body team up to tell us to inhale through an open mouth. The jaw then opens widely, which allows air in and out of the inner ear. Next, we exhale. **Yawning is also contagious between dogs and their owners.** Just hearing an owner yawn is enough to cause your furry friend to do the same.

Instant Genius
A yawn lasts about six seconds.

NOW YOU KNOW!
Birds, mammals, reptiles, and even some sharks yawn! And yawning is also contagious among chimpanzees.

146

#70

True or False:

Animals have held

public office.

I'm a political animal.

A CAT NAMED STUBBS SERVED AS THE HONORARY MAYOR OF TALKEETNA, ALASKA, U.S.A., FOR 20 YEARS. The orange tabby kitten was discovered in a box in the parking lot at the town's general store in 1997. The owner of the store adopted the kitten and **named him Stubbs because he didn't have a tail.** But the absence of a tail did not stop Stubbs from having a long career in politics! He was chosen to be the honorary mayor. Because the town was only a historic district, **Stubbs wasn't responsible for any important decisions,** but he did become a beloved tourist attraction.

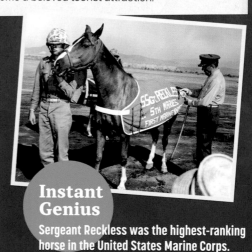

Instant Genius

Sergeant Reckless was the highest-ranking horse in the United States Marine Corps.

Where is the rainiest place on Earth?

a. India

b. Hawaii

c. Brazil

ANSWER: a India

IF YOU HAPPEN TO BE PLANNING A TRIP TO THE STATE OF MEGHALAYA, INDIA, PACK YOUR UMBRELLA: It's reportedly the rainiest place on the planet. The village of Mawsynram in Meghalaya receives an average of **467 inches (1,186 cm) of rain per year.** This heavy rainfall is due to summer air currents sweeping over the steaming-hot floodplains of Bangladesh, to its south. **The currents gather moisture as they move north, becoming big, fat clouds.** When those clouds hit the steep hills of Meghalaya, they are "squeezed" through the narrowed gap in the atmosphere until they can no longer hold the water. Then, the clouds release huge amounts of rain.

Instant Genius

The Dry Valleys area of Antarctica is the driest place on Earth. No rain has fallen there for nearly 2 million years.

Hills of Meghalaya

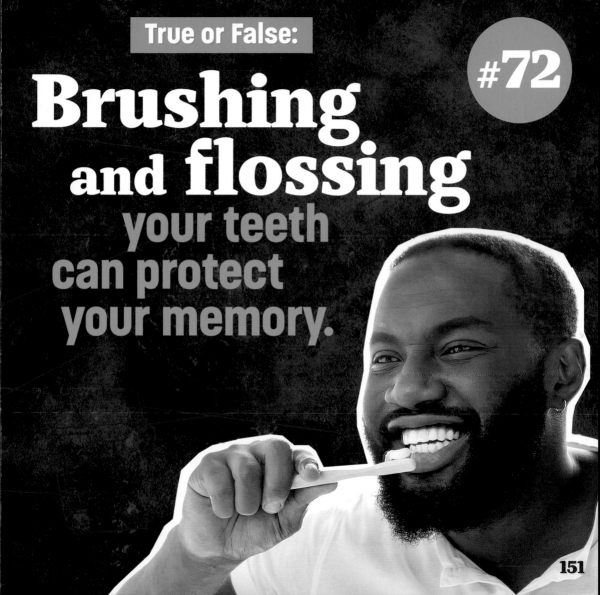

True or False:

Brushing and flossing your teeth can protect your memory.

#72

151

ANSWER: True

IT'S IMPORTANT TO TAKE CARE OF YOUR CHOMPERS.
Brushing and flossing twice a day helps remove plaque, a sticky, pale film that grows on the mouth's surfaces. Plaque—which forms from a combination of food, saliva, and fluids—**contains bacteria that can cause cavities, yellow teeth, and bad breath.** But neglecting to keep your teeth clean can create problems outside your mouth, too. When plaque gets stuck between your teeth and along the gum line, it can cause gum disease. **Experts have found that gum disease can move from the mouth to the brain** and damage nerve cells, which can then lead to memory loss.

Instant Genius

Tooth enamel (the outer surface of your teeth) is the hardest substance in the human body.

What do humans and zebras have in common?

#73

a. they're both mammals

b. they're both striped

c. they're both striped mammals

153

they are both striped mammals

YOU MIGHT BE SURPRISED TO LEARN THAT HUMANS AND ZEBRAS BOTH HAVE STRIPES. A zebra's stripes are easy to see; a human's are not. **Known as Blaschko's lines, they follow the same pattern on all people:** They curve around the body's sides, like tiger stripes, and rise in a swirl on the chest and upper back. They then dip down into a "V" shape along the spine and the middle of the chest. These lines also run up and down the arms and legs and along the face, above and below the eyes, and over the ears, kind of like painted-on glasses.

NOW YOU KNOW!
In rare cases, Blaschko's lines are visible. Usually, they can only be seen under black or ultraviolet light.

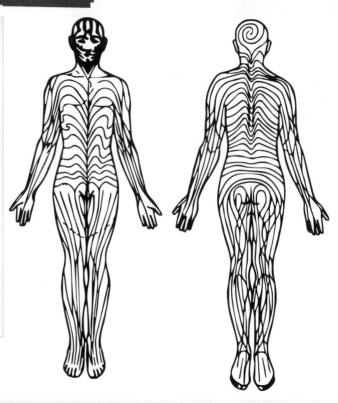

How much of the ocean is **unexplored?**

#74

a. 10 percent

b. 50 percent

c. 95 percent

155

ANSWER: **c** **95 percent**

WE KNOW MORE ABOUT THE SURFACES OF THE MOON AND MARS THAN WE DO ABOUT THE BOTTOM OF THE OCEAN. Why? Their surfaces are lit by the sun, and we can study them through satellite images. The ocean floor, however, is pitch black and hard to reach, so scientists have had to find other ways to explore it. Using ships equipped with mapping machines, **they send sound waves into the water.** If the sound waves hit an object, they bounce back; this sends a signal to the ship that something is there. **Only about one-fifth of the ocean has been mapped in high resolution.**

Instant Genius

The snailfish lives deeper in the ocean than any other fish known—at depths of 27,000 feet (8,230 m)!

True or False:

Horses can't

sleep standing up.

#75

Zzzzz

NOW YOU KNOW!
Horses need only two or three hours of sleep a day. They usually sleep for 15 minutes at a time.

Instant Genius
Zebras, elephants, and cows can also sleep standing up.

ANSWER: **False**

HORSES HAVE THE HANDY ABILITY TO SLEEP STANDING UP THANKS TO A BUILT-IN "HAMMOCK" INSIDE THEIR BODIES. A system of tendons and ligaments lock a horse's legs in position so the horse can sleep without falling over. A horse also uses its built-in hammock to rest its muscles when it is awake. **So how can you tell if a horse is sleeping? Look closely at its back legs.** One leg will be stiff, locked into place. The other back leg will be raised just a bit, and the very tip of the hoof will touch the ground. **Horses also sleep lying down, especially when they feel safe and warm.**

#76

True or False:

One-quarter
of the world's
hazelnuts
are used
in Nutella.

ANSWER: True

ABOUT 25 PERCENT OF THE WORLD'S YEARLY HAZELNUT SUPPLY WINDS UP IN NUTELLA, a creamy spread combining roasted hazelnuts, skim milk, and cocoa. **Nutella was invented during World War II** by an Italian chocolate-maker named Pietro Ferrero. Times were tough and Ferrero couldn't get enough cocoa, so he mixed in some ground hazelnuts. Ferrero originally made his chocolate-hazelnut paste into **a sliceable and spreadable loaf,** then later perfected the recipe to create the soft and creamy version we have today.

Instant Genius
Farmers have been growing hazelnuts for more than 2,000 years.

Unripe hazelnuts

What did Supreme Court Justice #77 Ruth Bader Ginsburg and rapper Notorious B.I.G. have in common?

a. They were both lawyers.

b. They were both from Brooklyn, New York.

c. They were both fans of opera.

ANSWER: b

They were both from Brooklyn, New York.

RUTH BADER GINSBURG WAS THE SECOND WOMAN TO BE APPOINTED TO THE SUPREME COURT, after Sandra Day O'Connor. She was also the first Jewish woman on the court. She spent her entire career fighting for women's rights and equality. For this, **she was dubbed Notorious R.B.G., a pun on the name of the rapper Notorious B.I.G.** When asked about the comparison, Ginsburg acknowledged that it **"seems altogether natural,"** as they were both born and raised in Brooklyn, New York.

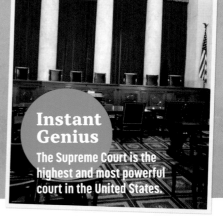

Instant Genius
The Supreme Court is the highest and most powerful court in the United States.

Which is the #78
coldest?

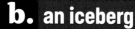
b. an iceberg

a. space

c. the outside of an airplane

163

DID YOU KNOW THAT AN ICEBERG IS ROUGHLY THE SAME TEMPERATURE AS ICE CREAM? Still, both are far warmer than the average air temperature outside an airplane flying at 30,000 feet (9,100 m). At that altitude, it can be as low as -70°F (-57°C). While that might sound really chilly, it doesn't compare to the frigid temperatures in space. Astronomers say **the Boomerang Nebula is the coldest-known object in the universe,** with a temperature of **-458°F (-272°C).** The Boomerang Nebula, like all nebulae, is a cloud of gas and dust.

Instant Genius

The Boomerang Nebula is also known as the Bowtie Nebula because of its shape.

True or False:

Some animals can

walk on water.

#79

165

ANSWER: True

INSECTS, REPTILES, BIRDS, AND EVEN MAMMALS HAVE DEVELOPED THIS SUPERPOWER. They do it to escape from predators on land and to find food. **There are two different types of water-walking animals: gliders and slappers.** Most gliders, such as **water striders, are tiny insects** that are light on their feet. Being lightweight allows gliders to be supported by the surface of the water. Larger water walkers are slappers. The surface of water is too weak to hold their heavier bodies, so slappers need speed, momentum, and strength to stay afloat. The **basilisk lizard,** for example, slaps water, creating tiny air pockets with its hind feet. It swiftly crosses over water before the air pockets close.

Look, Ma, no flippers!

NOW YOU KNOW!
Bottlenose dolphins are one of the few mammals that can "walk" on water. They beat their tails back and forth to help lift their bodies up. Then they move forward with only their tails still under the surface.

How big was the first cell phone?

#80

a. nearly 1 foot (0.3 m) long

b. 1 pound (0.5 kg)

c. nearly 8 pounds (3.6 kg)

nearly 1 foot (0.3 m) long

THE WORLD'S FIRST CELL PHONE CALL WAS MADE IN APRIL 1973. But this cell phone was nothing like the ones we have today. It was about the size of a shoebox and **weighed 2.5 pounds (1.1 kg).** That's about six times heavier than today's typical cell phone. **It also took 10 hours to recharge** after a 35-minute call. In addition to being heavy, clunky, and energy inefficient, the phone was also **expensive at $4,000.** That would be the equivalent of about $10,000 today! Cell phones have come a long way since 1973. Today's cell phones have more power than the computer used for the Apollo 11 moon landing!

Instant Genius

More people in the world have a cell phone than have a toilet.

168

Insects

#81

are commonly eaten
throughout the world.

ANSWER: True

INSECTS ARE CONSIDERED A TASTY TREAT IN MANY COUNTRIES. In Mexico, fried grasshoppers are sold in markets as a crunchy snack. In the Asian countries of China and Thailand, insects such as **crickets and ants are slathered in chocolate** and savored. In southern Africa, caterpillars are a regular part of some people's diet. Not only are insects **packed with healthy nutrients, including protein and fiber,** but eating them instead of meat is also **healthier for the planet,** according to many experts. Why? Insects don't use up a lot of natural resources like water and land for grazing on grass.

Which of the following is true about Abraham Lincoln?

#82

a. He led the country through the American Civil War, ending slavery.

b. He is featured in the Wrestling Hall of Fame.

c. Both A and B.

ANSWER: C

Both A and B.

ABRAHAM LINCOLN WAS THE 16TH PRESIDENT OF THE UNITED STATES. He is credited with leading the nation through its most difficult period: the American Civil War, which lasted from 1861 to 1865. Thanks to Lincoln's leadership, **slavery was abolished and the Union was preserved.** What is less known about Lincoln is that, at age 21, **he was a wrestling champion in his home county in Illinois.** Defeated only once in 300 matches, he earned the title "Outstanding American" in the Wrestling Hall of Fame.

83

True or False:

A goldfish will **turn pale without enough sunlight.**

let there be light!

173

ANSWER: **True**

GOLDFISH CAN BE YELLOW, ORANGE, RED, BROWN, OR BLACK. To keep their colors, they need sunlight. Why? Special cells in their bodies produce **pigments that reflect the light that makes them so colorful.** Without sunlight falling on these pigments, a goldfish's color could fade, making it look pale. **Goldfish can also change color depending** on water temperature and on their age.

Instant Genius

Tish, the world's longest-lived goldfish, survived for 43 years.

Which of these is the **tallest building** in the world?

a. Eiffel Tower in Paris, France

b. Burj Khalifa in Dubai, United Arab Emirates

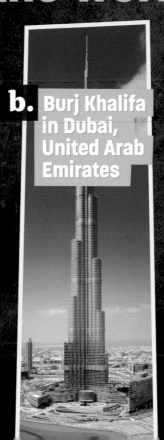

#84

c. Shanghai Tower in Shanghai, China

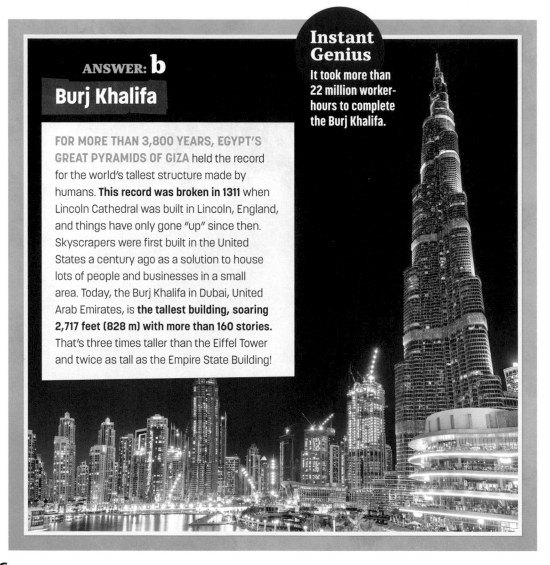

ANSWER: b

Burj Khalifa

Instant Genius

It took more than 22 million worker-hours to complete the Burj Khalifa.

FOR MORE THAN 3,800 YEARS, EGYPT'S GREAT PYRAMIDS OF GIZA held the record for the world's tallest structure made by humans. **This record was broken in 1311** when Lincoln Cathedral was built in Lincoln, England, and things have only gone "up" since then. Skyscrapers were first built in the United States a century ago as a solution to house lots of people and businesses in a small area. Today, the Burj Khalifa in Dubai, United Arab Emirates, is **the tallest building, soaring 2,717 feet (828 m) with more than 160 stories.** That's three times taller than the Eiffel Tower and twice as tall as the Empire State Building!

True or False: You are made up mostly of **water.**

#85

177

ANSWER: True

YOU ARE MADE FROM SMALL BUILDING BLOCKS CALLED CELLS, WHICH ARE ABOUT 70 PERCENT WATER. The water in your blood helps carry important nutrients and oxygen to all the cells in your body. Water also helps the human body **release heat through sweating,** which cools the skin and regulates body temperature. That's why **it's really important to hydrate on superhot days** or when playing sports—to replenish the water you need to keep your body functioning.

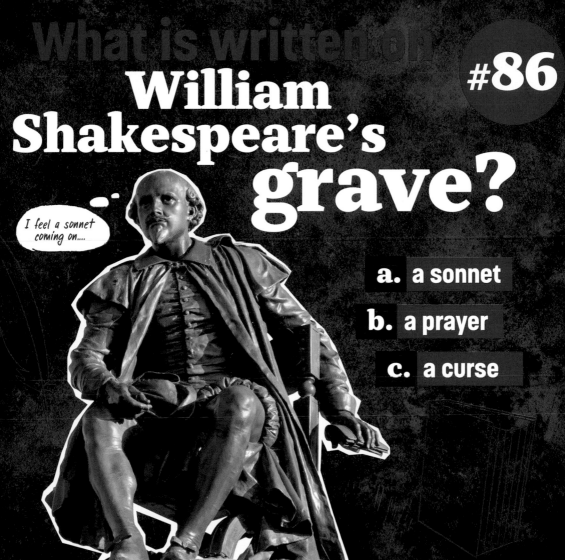

179

ANSWER: C

a curse

DURING THE 17TH CENTURY, WILLIAM SHAKESPEARE WROTE FAMOUS PLAYS such as *Romeo and Juliet* and *Hamlet*. Before Shakespeare died in April 1616, he knew he would be **buried beneath a stone slab inside a church.** Still, he worried about grave robbers, who were common then. To scare off thieves, Shakespeare **wrote a curse to be left on his grave to discourage potential robbers from stealing.** The curse didn't scare off everyone, however. Archaeologists who were studying Shakespeare's grave made a startling discovery: **His skull appears to be missing.**

Instant Genius

Shakespeare's parents, and likely his own children, never learned to read or write.

GOOD FREND FOR JESVS SAKE FORBEARE,
TO DIGG THE DVST ENCLOASED HEARE.
BLESE BE Y MAN T SPARES THES STONES,
AND CVRST BE HE Y MOVES MY BONES.

GOOD FRIEND FOR JESUS' SAKE FORBEAR,
TO DIG THE DUST ENCLOSED HERE.
BLESSED BE THE MAN THAT SPARES THESE STONES,
AND CURSED BE HE THAT MOVES MY BONES.
Shakespeare's Gravestone - Holy Trinity Stratford-upon-Avon

AN EXCELLENT conceited Tragedie OF Romeo and Iuliet.
As it hath been often (with great applause) plaid publiquely, by the right Honourable the L. of Hunsdon his Seruants.
LONDON,
Printed by Iohn Danter.
1597

THE Tragicall Historie of HAMLET, Prince of Denmarke.
By William Shakespeare.
Newly imprinted and enlarged to almost as much againe as it was, according to the true and perfect Coppie.
AT LONDON,
Printed by I.R. for N.L. and are to be sold at his shoppe under Saint Dunstons Church in Fleetstreet. 1605.

THE GRAVE
OF THE POET
WILLIAM
SHAKESPEARE
1564-1616

How long was the world's longest tennis match?

#87

a. 3 hours

b. 6 hours

c. 11 hours

ANSWER: C

11 hours

EACH YEAR, THE BEST TENNIS PLAYERS IN THE WORLD COMPETE IN FOUR TOURNAMENTS CALLED THE GRAND SLAM. One of those is Wimbledon, which began in 1877 and is **the world's oldest tennis tournament.** In 2010, two players—John Isner of the United States and Nicolas Mahut of France—faced off in **a match at Wimbledon that took three days to complete.** It went on for so long that the scoreboard malfunctioned! Tennis fans around the world tuned in to see what would happen next. Finally, after 11 hours and 5 minutes of playing time, **Isner, the 25-year-old American, won the match.**

Instant Genius

The previous record for the longest tennis match was 4 hours and 3 minutes.

#88

True or False:

The
ostrich
and the
T. rex
are related.

183

ANSWER: **True**

IN 2005, PALEONTOLOGISTS FOUND GIANT DINOSAUR BONES IN A FIELD IN MONTANA. To fit the huge leg bone—called the femur—onto a helicopter to take it to the lab, it had to be broken into pieces. This was a very lucky break! From inside the femur, **researchers removed molecules of collagen,** a protein that gives bones structure. Scientists **compared the dinosaur collagen with the collagen of other living animals,** including humans, chickens, ostriches—and even salmon. Of the more than 20 animals they compared it with, *T. rex*'s collagen was the **most similar to chickens and ostriches.**

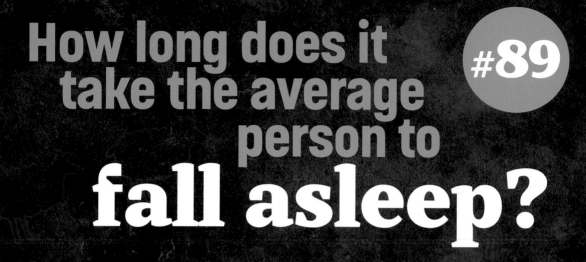

How long does it take the average person to **fall asleep?**

#89

a. 2 minutes

b. 10 to 20 minutes

c. 45 minutes

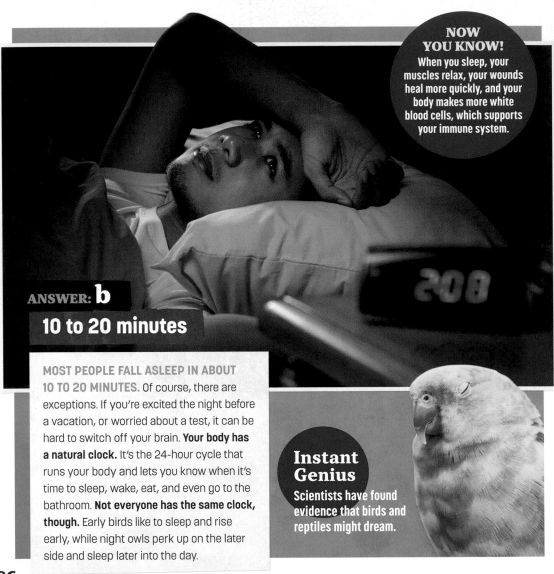

ANSWER: b

10 to 20 minutes

MOST PEOPLE FALL ASLEEP IN ABOUT 10 TO 20 MINUTES. Of course, there are exceptions. If you're excited the night before a vacation, or worried about a test, it can be hard to switch off your brain. **Your body has a natural clock.** It's the 24-hour cycle that runs your body and lets you know when it's time to sleep, wake, eat, and even go to the bathroom. **Not everyone has the same clock, though.** Early birds like to sleep and rise early, while night owls perk up on the later side and sleep later into the day.

Instant Genius
Scientists have found evidence that birds and reptiles might dream.

186

Which of these dog breeds is considered the most intelligent?

a. border collie

b. beagle

c. bulldog

border collie

POODLES, GERMAN SHEPHERDS, AND GOLDEN RETRIEVERS ALL GET HIGH MARKS IN THE SMARTS DEPARTMENT, but the award for most intelligent dog breed goes to the border collie. Border collies learn quickly and are stars when it comes to following directions. **Chaser, a border collie from South Carolina, U.S.A.,** could identify and retrieve more than 1,000 different toys by name. She was also **able to recognize adjectives—words that describe something—** so she could understand directions to fetch a "bigger" or "smaller" ball.

Chaser

#91

True or False:

Hot water **freezes faster** than cold water.

ANSWER: **True**

THIS WAS PROVED WHEN A HIGH SCHOOL STUDENT FROM TANZANIA, a country in Africa, conducted **a science experiment with a bit of a twist.** The student was making ice cream. Instead of waiting for his mixture to cool, **he put it in the freezer while it was still hot.** Surprisingly, the ice cream froze faster than the mixtures of his classmates, who had allowed theirs to cool first. **Scientists are still not sure exactly why hot water freezes faster than cold water.** One theory has to do with water molecules. A chemical bond occurs when water molecules cling together. In cold water, some bonds are weak, others are strong. The weak bonds break to form ice crystals. Hot water has fewer weak bonds, so it can form ice crystals faster.

When Hawaii and Alaska were admitted to the United States, who redesigned the American flag?

#92

a. Betsy Ross

b. a high school junior

c. First Lady Mamie Eisenhower

191

President Eisenhower unveiling the new flag

Dear president Eisenhower,
My name is Sheryl Brylard. I am 8 years old.
My sugjestion for the new flag for the 49th states.

I'm sorry to disturb you.
sheryl

One of the submissions that wasn't chosen

ANSWER: b

a high school junior

SINCE IT WAS DESIGNED IN 1775, THE AMERICAN FLAG HAS BEEN CHANGED TO ADD STATES JOINING THE UNION. Different versions had stars arranged into various shapes, including a circle, a diamond, and even a star. In 1959, when Alaska became state 49 and Hawaii became state 50, **President Eisenhower received thousands of ideas for how update the flag.** A high school junior from Ohio submitted a version he had made for a class project. **His design was accepted and is still used today.**

#93

What killed the dinosaurs?

a. other animals

b. an asteroid

c. prehistoric humans

Yikes!

ANSWER: b

an asteroid

IN THE 1980S, SCIENTISTS FOUND THE ELEMENT IRIDIUM IN A LAYER OF CLAY THAT DATED BACK 66 MILLION YEARS, the same time dinosaurs went extinct. Iridium is abundant in asteroids, so the discovery of iridium in this layer of rock made the scientists think that maybe an asteroid hit Earth, killing the dinosaurs. **A decade later a gigantic crater was discovered off the coast of the Yucatán Peninsula in Mexico.** It also dated to the same time dinosaurs went extinct. This discovery supported the scientists' theory. **The asteroid impact likely caused wildfires, tsunamis, earthquakes, and volcanic eruptions,** sending dust into the sky and turning Earth dark. Many plants and animals would have died out—including the dinosaurs.

Instant Genius
Dinosaurs roamed Earth for nearly 200 million years.

True or False: Trees can

communicate

with one another.

#94

ANSWER: **True**

WE KNOW THAT ANIMALS HAVE WAYS OF COMMUNICATING WITH ONE ANOTHER, and scientists have discovered that trees do, too. Experts call this quiet connection the "wood wide web," and they believe it links 90 percent of trees and fungi. Trees share information and resources with one another through a detailed network of fungi and bacteria—teeny, tiny organisms known as microbes. Millions of microbe species exchange nutrients through the soil and roots of trees. Older trees share sugars with younger trees, and sick trees will even send any nutrients they have back to their network for other trees to take in before they die.

Instant Genius

Trees can warn each other about dangers such as insect infestations.

How fast #95
does a storm's wind speed need to be to be classified as a

hurricane?

a. 74 miles an hour (119 kmh)

b. 65 miles an hour (105 kmh)

c. 35 miles an hour (56 kmh)

74 miles an hour (119 kmh)

HURRICANES START AS TROPICAL STORMS OVER THE OCEAN, NEAR THE EQUATOR. When warm, moist air over the water rises, it is replaced by cooler air. The cooler air warms and starts to rise. If there is enough warm water, **the cycle will continue creating more storm clouds and faster winds.** This causes a hurricane to form. To be considered a hurricane, a tropical storm's wind speed must reach at least 74 miles an hour (119 kmh). **The strongest hurricanes produce winds of more than 157 miles an hour (252 kmh).** Along with heavy winds, a typical hurricane brings lots of rain, too.

Instant Genius

Hurricanes spin counterclockwise in the Northern Hemisphere and clockwise in the Southern Hemisphere.

True or False:

You can find out the temperature by counting **a cricket's chirps.**

#96

199

I'm a rock star.

ANSWER: **True**

THERE ARE ABOUT 2,400 SPECIES OF CRICKETS, AND EACH MAKES ITS OWN UNIQUE CHIRPING SOUND. The speed at which a cricket chirps changes depending on how hot or cold it is. By listening to a cricket's chirps, you can roughly estimate the temperature: **Count the number of chirps in 15 seconds, then add 37.** That number should be close to the outside temperature. **Crickets chirp more in warmer weather** because warmer weather makes it easier for crickets to rub their wings together. This motion is what makes the chirping sound. Male crickets are usually the "singers," and they use their chirps to attract mates.

Instant Genius
Male crickets have a playlist of songs and will choose one depending on how close or far a potential mate is.

#97

You can tell a horse is **smiling** by looking at what part of its body?

a. its ears **b.** its mouth **c.** its tail

Cheese!

its ears

WANT TO KNOW WHAT A HORSE IS FEELING? Look at its ears! **Horses have 10 different muscles in each ear.** These muscles allow horses to rotate their ears 180 degrees (that's half a rotation around a circle), which gives them a lot of flexibility to express themselves. **Horses "smile" by pricking their ears forward.** When a horse tips its ears back, it may be telling us it's bored. And if a horse's ears are flat against its head, this can mean it's angry. **Scientists have found that horses can make 17 different facial expressions** and that they use their ear positions to send messages to other horses.

Instant Genius

People have 43 muscles in their face that they can use to make more than 10,000 facial expressions.

#98

True or False:

You are
taller
in space.

THE REASON IS GRAVITY. When a person is standing on Earth, gravity pulls the body's fluids down toward the feet. There is fluid in discs between the bones of the spine, which keep the spine straight. So gravity pulls that liquid down, too, and **squishes those discs closer together, making us shorter.** In space there is nearly zero gravity, so an astronaut's body fluids go toward her head. With no weight pulling the bones of the spine down, they expand. This makes **astronauts in space up to three percent taller.** That means a 5.5-foot (1.7 m)-tall person could gain almost 2 inches (5 cm) in space!

Instant Genius

It takes about one month for an astronaut to return to their normal height once back on Earth.

NOW YOU KNOW!

You are slightly taller when you wake up in the morning than when you go to bed at night.

#99

True or False:

The first passengers on a hot-air balloon were **a duck, a sheep, and a rooster.**

THE FIRST HOT-AIR BALLOON WAS LAUNCHED IN 1783 WITH A DUCK, A ROOSTER, AND A SHEEP ABOARD. Before sending humans into flight, the inventors—**French brothers Joseph-Michel and Jacques-Étienne Montgolfier—wanted to see how different animals would respond.** They chose a duck because ducks have the ability to fly at higher altitudes and wouldn't be harmed. The rooster was chosen to see how a bird that can fly only at very low altitudes would handle being in the sky. And the sheep joined the birds because it's a land animal and would give the brothers **a sense of what it would be like for people flying in the balloon.**

Instant Genius

When it was first launched, the hot-air balloon flew for 8 minutes and traveled 2 miles (3.2 km) before landing safely.

NOW YOU KNOW!

Today, balloons are also used for scientific investigation. They help scientists study the inside of hurricanes and one day may set sail to Venus, Mars, or Saturn.

How many
people
live on Earth?

#100

a. nearly 7 billion

b. nearly 8 billion

c. nearly 9 billion

開往车公庄方向
To CHEGONGZHUANG

开往积水潭方向
To JISHUITAN

ANSWER: b

nearly 8 billion

THE TOTAL NUMBER OF PEOPLE ON EARTH IS ESTIMATED TO BE NEARLY 8 BILLION. It took more than 200,000 years of human history for the world's population to reach 1 billion and only 200 years to reach 8 billion—and the number is still growing. **By 2050, 9.7 billion people are expected to inhabit the globe.** By 2100, Earth's population is projected to grow to 11 billion. **The most populated country in the world is China.** India has the second-largest population, followed by the United States, which has the third largest.

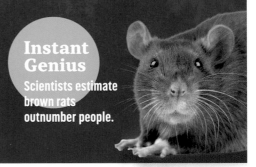

Instant Genius
Scientists estimate brown rats outnumber people.

True or False:

Ancient Egyptians #101

kept cats as pets.

Mummy, where are you?

ANSWER: **True**

FOUR THOUSAND YEARS AGO, CATS WERE POPULAR IN ANCIENT EGYPTIAN CULTURE. Believed to bring good luck, they were included in social gatherings and religious events. **They were praised for killing venomous snakes** and protecting pharaohs (rulers). Egyptians also worshiped a cat goddess and **even mummified their pets for their journey to the afterlife.** If one of their beloved kitties died before them, ancient Egyptians would **shave off their eyebrows in mourning.**

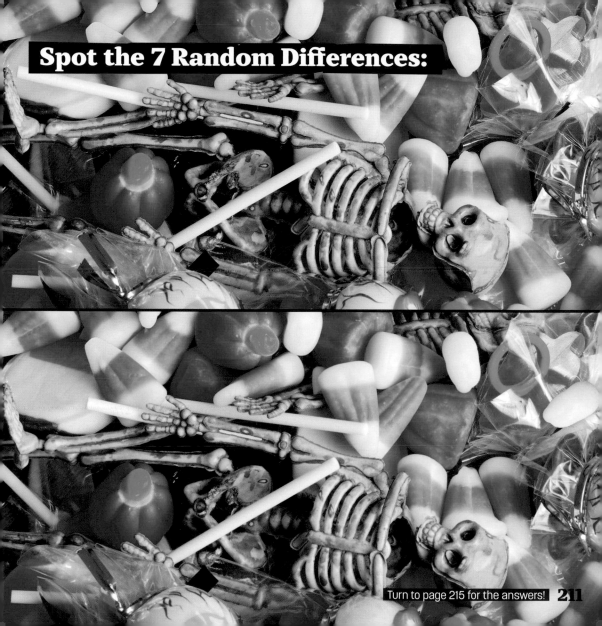

Spot the 7 Random Differences:

Turn to page 215 for the answers!

Index

Page numbers in *italic* refer to images.

Photo Credits

The publishers would like to thank the following for the use of their images. While every effort has been made to credit images, the publishers will be pleased to correct any errors or omissions in future editions of the book.

t = top; b = bottom; l = left; r = right; c = center

123rf.com: pp. 38(br), 132(br).

Alamy: pp. 24(t), 40(t,br), 84(t), 102(cr), 104, 120(br), 161(br), 167, 172(l), 182, 206(l).

Pilley Bianchi: p. 188(br).

docuteach.org: p. 192(bl).

Dreamstime: pp. 1, 2(tl,br), 4, 5(tcr), 6(t,l), 7(bl,cr), 10(t,br), 11, 12(t,br), 13, 14(t,br), 15, 16(t,br), 17, 18(t,br), 19(cl,cr,bl), 20(tr,b), 21, 22(t,br), 23, 24(t), 25, 26(tl,cr), 27(t,b), 28, 29, 30, 31, 33, 34(t,br), 35 (l,bc,r), 36(t,br), 37, 38(t), 39, 41 (tr,cr,bl,br), 42(tl,tr,br), 43(tr,cr,bl), 44(t,cl), 45, 46(t,br), 49, 50(t,br), 51, 52(t,br), 53, 54(l,bc), 57, 58(t,br), 60(t,br), 61, 62(t,br), 63(bl,br), 64, 67, 68(t), 69, 70(br), 71(cl,c,br), 72(t,br), 75, 76(t), 79, 80(t,br), 81, 83(cr,bl), 84(bcr), 86(tl,br), 88(tl,bl), 89, 90(br), 91, 92, 94(tl,tr), 95, 96(tr), 98, 99, 100(t,br), 101, 102(t), 105(cl,bl,br), 106(l,br), 107(bl,bc,br), 108, 109, 110, 111, 112(tr,b), 113, 114, 115, 116(l), 117, 118(t,bl), 119, 120(t), 121, 122, 123(bl,bc,br), 124(t,br), 125, 126(t), 127, 128(l,br), 129(bl,br), 130(br), 131(all), 132(tl,tr), 133, 134(t), 135(l,c,r), 136(t,br), 137, 138, 139, 140(t,br), 141, 142(b), 145, 146(bl,r), 147, 149(l,bc,r), 150(tr), 151, 152(t,br), 153, 155, 157, 159(t,br), 160(l,bc), 162(t), 163(c,br), 165, 166(tl,br), 169, 170(t,br), 171, 172(tr), 173, 174, 175(l,c,r), 176, 177, 178, 179, 180(main photo), 181(all), 183(tl,r), 184(t,br), 185, 186(t,br), 187(bl,bc,br), 188(l), 189, 190(t,bl), 191, 193, 194, 195, 196(t,br), 197, 199, 200, 201, 205, 206(br), 207, 208(t,br), 209, 210(br), 211(t,b), 215.

ESA (European Space Agency) © ESA/NASA: p. 90(t).

Mackenzie Gerringer, PhD, SUNY Geneseo (State University of New York at Geneseo): p. 156(bcr).

Getty Images: pp. 47, 48, 73, 74, 150(b), 161(bl), 168.

Heritage Auctions, HA.com: p. 82(cr).

iStockphoto: pp. 24(br), 59, 65, 66, 68(t), 85, 87, 96(l), 158, 202.

Library of Congress: pp. 82(t), 103, 162(br).

Metropolitan Museum of Art, New York: pp. 68(br/Gift of Collis P. Huntington, 1897), 210(tl/Rogers Fund 1930).

NASA (National Aeronautics and Space Administration): pp. 5(cl), 8–9, 32(bl,r), 55, 56, 63(c), 77, 78(t,br), 93, 94(br), 97, 134(br), 143, 144(bl,cl,r), 163(bl), 164, 198, 203, 204.

Nature Picture Library: pp. 70(t), 129(c), 130(l), 142(tl), 166(cr).

NOAA (National Oceanic and Atmospheric Administration/ OMAO Office of Marine and Aviation Operations): p. 156(t).

Shutterstock Editorial: pp. 148(l), 192(t).

ThunderWorks.com: p. 76(br).

US Marine Corps History Division: p. 148(br).

Wikimedia Commons: pp. 116(br), 126(bl), 180(tr).

Credits

Text and cover design copyright © 2022 by
Penguin Random House LLC

All rights reserved. Published in the United States by Random House
Children's Books, a division of Penguin Random House LLC, New York.

Random House and the colophon are registered trademarks of
Penguin Random House LLC.

Visit us on the Web! **rhcbooks.com**

Educators and librarians, for a variety of teaching tools, visit us
at **RHTeachersLibrarians.com**

Library of Congress Cataloging-in-Publication Data is available
upon request.
ISBN 978-0-593-45030-7 (trade)
ISBN 978-0-593-45036-9 (lib. bdg.)
ISBN 978-0-593-51611-9 (ebook)

COVER PHOTO CREDITS:
Front Cover Photo: Shutterstock.
Back Cover Photo: Dreamstime.

MANUFACTURED IN ITALY
10 9 8 7 6 5 4 3 2
First Edition

Penguin Random House LLC supports copyright. Copyright fuels
creativity, encourages diverse voices, promotes free speech,
and creates a vibrant culture. Thank you for buying an authorized
edition of this book and for complying with copyright laws by
not reproducing, scanning, or distributing any part in any form
without permission. You are supporting writers and allowing
Penguin Random House to publish books for every reader.

Produced by Fun Factory Press, LLC, in association with
Potomac Global Media, LLC.

The publisher would like to thank the following people for their
contributions to this book: Melina Gerosa Bellows, President,
Fun Factory Press, and Series Creator and Author; Priyanka
Lamichhane, Editor and Project Manager; Chad Tomlinson, Art
Director; Jen Agresta, Copy Editor; Michelle Harris, Fact-checker;
Potomac Global Media: Kevin Mulroy, Publisher; Barbara Brownell
Grogan, Editor-in-Chief, Thomas Keenes, Designer; Susannah
Jayes and Ellen Dupont, Picture Researchers; Jane Sunderland,
Proofreader.

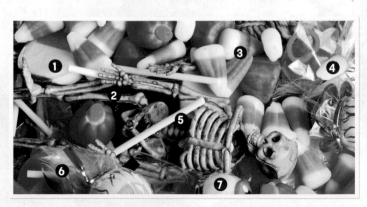

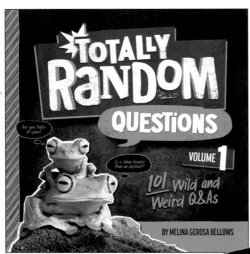